TENURED

TENURED

THE SINGLE GREATEST THREAT TO HIGHER EDUCATION?

2ND EDITION

MITCHELL L. SPRINGER

Niche Pressworks
Indianapolis, IN

Copyright © 2026 by Mitchell L. Springer

All rights reserved.

DISCLAIMER

The views and opinions expressed in this book are those of the author and do not in any way reflect the official policy, position, or views of any specific university. Examples of analysis performed within this book are only examples and should not be utilized in real-world analytic products or processes as they are based only on limited and current date open source information. This information is provided and sold with the knowledge that the publisher and author do not offer any legal or other professional advice. In the case of a need for any such expertise consult with the appropriate professional. This book does not contain all information available on the subject. This book has not been created to be specific to any individuals' or organizations' situation or needs. Although the author and publisher have made every effort to ensure that the information in this book was correct at press time, the author and publisher do not assume and hereby disclaim any liability to any party for any loss, damage, or disruption caused by errors or omissions, whether such errors or omissions result from negligence, accident, or any other cause. The information contained within this book is provided for informational purposes only, and should not be construed as legal advice on any matter. Recipients of information contained herein should not act upon this information without seeking professional counsel.

ISBN: 978-1-962956-85-7

Cover design by Michael Panich

Editorial work by Robyn Smith

Published by Niche Pressworks; NichePressworks.com
Indianapolis, IN

Table of Contents

Prologue	vii
Introduction	**1**
American Higher Education is Broken	1
The Winds of Change	12
A Word of Intent before Proceeding	27
Truth #1: Protecting What Does Not Have an Economic Right to Exist; 45+ Years of Unsustainable Liability	**29**
Recessions and Unemployment	39
Oversupply of Tenured Professors in the Academy	43
Who are Today's College Students	54
Implications of our Understanding of this Generational Cohort	81
The Formation of Unions and their Purpose	81
Why Tenure Exists	88
Why Tenure Fails the Taxpayer	96
Truth #2: Implications of Entitlement; No Burning Platform, No Sense of Urgency	**127**
Community Colleges Begin Offering Bachelor Degrees Across US	144
The Politics of Entitlement	146
Fear – From Paralysis to Power	148
Truth #3: Tenure as a Closed System: Coercion, Groupthink, Bias and Inherently Discriminatory	**157**
Quantitative and Qualitative Elements of Decision Making	159
Business Case for Diversity and Inclusivity: It's All about Growth	167
Closed Versus Open Systems	173

    How the Tenure Process Contributes to Coercion,
        Groupthink and Prejudice   176

Addressing Those Questions Which are the Essence of the Argument   183
    How Do We Attract the Best and Brightest?   183
    How Do We Keep People From Leaving?   193
    How Do We Ensure Faculty Can Teach as They
        Feel Appropriate?   201
    How Do We Create Excellence in a Given Discipline?   206
    Without Tenure, How Do I Find a Job if Something
        Happens to Me?   207
    The Academy is Not a Business!   208
    The Elimination of Tenure Would be Catastrophic
        to Higher Education!   215

Alternative Solutions to Tenure   217
    Unionization   218
    Contract Term-Limits   220
    Simply Phasing It Out   225
    Mediating to a Successful Resolution   226

Conclusion   233
    There Are No Problems in Academia That Have
        Not Already Been Solved   233
    Guaranteed Lifetime Employment Runs Counter to Three
        Basic Tenants of Efficiency and Cost Containment   244

Bibliography   251

About the Author   289

Prologue

I have roughly 45 books on my shelves and hundreds of applicable articles, written by College/University Presidents, past Presidents, Provosts, faculty, staff and others that offer insights and perceptions on how to fix higher education.

Given this, the content of this book provides over 30 years of synthesized evidence in support of a position on changing tenure practices in public institutions of higher education. It has been scrubbed such that there are no stories associated with any one university, as well as any classified or competition sensitive information.

In short, of all the potential opportunities in academia to increase efficiency and reduce costs, the one which stands out as the elephant in the room, the one seldom mentioned, the single largest impediment to transforming public institutions of higher education, is guaranteed lifetime employment (pronounced *tenure*).

The literature clearly suggests tenure runs counter to three undeniable and indisputable basic tenants of being good stewards of taxpayer dollars and student tuition.

1. Tenure creates an unjustifiable and unsustainable long-term financial commitment on the part of the college/university (45+ years).
2. Tenure creates a sense of entitlement, which aggressively (negatively) reacts to the creation of efficiencies and attendant cost reductions.
3. As a process, tenure is biased, prejudicial and widely acknowledged as being inherently discriminatory.

I sincerely believe this is a topic for the National agenda.

Introduction

American Higher Education is Broken

> *Like another American icon, the auto industry in Detroit, the higher education industry is beset by hubris, opposition to change, and resistance to accountability. Even the leaders of colleges and universities think we are in trouble...higher education is clinging to tradition. Too few students are going to college, not enough are graduating, and the whole thing costs too much... (Selingo xi)*

While working in the defense industry for nearly thirty years, I was afforded the opportunity to be part of the transition management teams for five major mergers/acquisitions and significantly more restructurings. Being a part of these projects provided invaluable insight into how to find efficiencies. Depending on the discipline and efficiency focus of the product life cycle, there are hundreds of opportunities to reduce inefficiency and cost. These reductions provide a more effective and cost efficient output for the betterment of the organization, its shareholders, and its customers. Sometimes these efficiencies come in the form of centralizing policies, procedures, methodologies, and practices. Other times they come in the form of common software and hardware. Still other times they come in the form of inventory control and production efficiency. No matter where you look in the product or service lifecycle, there are ways to increase efficiency and reduce overall costs; this we have proven in business and industry many times, over hundreds of years.

In transitioning my career to academia, it became immediately obvious that there were significant inefficiencies, replicated resources, and no attention to return on investment (ROI). All these factors created woefully wasteful, exaggerated, and inflamed costs. What most surprised me was anyone from business/industry who was working in the academy saw the same things I saw. We would openly talk about the lack of stewardship of taxpayer money and student tuition. In most every case the conversation ended with statements along the lines of "…the waste and abuse should be a crime with prosecutions similar to Enron…"

Some of the more obvious problems seem simple to solve, such as reducing multiple mail server applications or having more than three dozen web design tools. To see how this manifests

INTRODUCTION

itself into cost drivers of inefficiency, look at the example of multiple web application design tools. Many academic units use a tool exclusive to that department. Consequently, they have the only people on campus capable of using that tool as well as maintaining the content and infrastructure of the tool's web designed pages. You can see how this creates a scenario of having to retain people specifically for the use of this isolated tool. In the least, it prohibits the cross-fertilization of web-designed pages from other units who use a different tool. The same problem can be seen from having multiple mail applications where one does not efficiently talk to the other. These examples are simply low hanging fruit when it comes to efficiency gains.

Colleges and universities are under increasing pressure to accomplish four things: increase revenues, decrease expenses, improve quality, and strengthen reputation (Dickeson, 1). This book deals directly with decreasing expenses. By doing so, we can fuel and promote changes in revenue, quality improvement, and a college's or university's reputation. *The intent of this book is to merely share observations, begin a conversation, and hopefully distil fears attendant to change.* Thus, the following discussion revolves around that which must happen in order to allow the transformation of public higher education.

In my research of nearly 25 years of literature, most every argument I have come across for not making the change proposed below stems entirely from fear. The once rational arguments put forth are no longer premised on current day realities.

Of all the potential opportunities in academia to increase efficiency and reduce costs, the one, which stands out as the elephant in the room; the one seldom mentioned; the single largest impediment to transforming public institutions of higher education; is guaranteed lifetime employment (pronounced *tenure*).

Dickeson discusses cost in his book, *Prioritizing Academic Programs and Services*:

> **The principle line-item expense in academic programs is personnel costs... the problem is exacerbated by overly generous tenure practices.** A large number of academic departments in the nation are "tenured up", where past tenure practice has filled every available personnel slot with a tenured faculty member, thus limiting flexibility in reducing positions. Additional pressures come from legal challenges to mandatory retirement policies. Faced with reducing costs in a labor-intensive enterprise like higher education and confronted by the extraordinary reluctance to move tenured faculty, many institutions feel hamstrung in their efforts to get control... it is time to recognize colleges and universities must get a better handle on expenses. To date, most of the effort has been to (1) focus on the administrative, nonacademic portions of the institution, (2) defer maintenance of the physical plant to the point that recovery

INTRODUCTION

becomes financially unfeasible, (3) ignore the academic program side as too politically volatile to touch, and (4) make necessary budget cuts across the board so that all programs suffer equally, which is politically expedient on campus but academically repugnant (23).

Tenure, for all the good that was intended with its creation, no longer has an economic or any other right to exist. The reasons for its creation may have been well founded, but those reasons are no longer applicable. Tenure has become a relic of the past which requires it be retired (no pun intended). There are no good reasons for tenure to exist in today's environment. *In fact,* ***guaranteed lifetime employment (tenure) is now the single largest obstacle to the transformation of public higher education.***

Tenure prohibits the very efficiencies required in today's dwindling financial support. Tenure creates more of an adversarial relationship than unionization ever did. Minimally, in a union environment, guaranteed lifetime employment is not an end goal. In fact, the very issuance of guaranteed lifetime employment promotes an unjustifiable sense of security from termination that runs counter to any and every attempt to run an efficient organizational unit. Lack of cooperation and unprofessional, immature behavior are just a few of the omnipresent and systemic cancerous behaviors of tenure.

Every stated reason for tenure to exist is really no longer valid. Also, it is easily shown that the actions required to transform public higher education are being directly inhibited by the tenure process and those individuals possessing the most to lose: tenured faculty.

The entire tenure system is devised to protect the status quo – those who want into it and those who belong to it. Yet at times, it violates cultural laws of morality and ethics by opposing those who want to change the academic environment to protect the concept of public higher education.

A very brief introduction into the tenure process clearly reflects its many issues. To become tenured, a non-tenured faculty member must remain silent against perceived challenges to faculty and tenure in servitude to those full professors who have direct influence over the non-tenured fate, and collusion against those who pose a challenge to the status quo.

Once a non-tenured faculty member has endured their seven years of servitude, they are voted on by their faculty superiors for acceptability into the tenured ranks.

The process is extremely subjective; it frequently leans to the loudest among those with voting privileges, and in the end may be determined simply by what is termed "collegiality" or "non-collegiality". In other words, did they like you? Anyone with any background in coercion, groupthink or the inclusivity of diversity can readily understand the primary cause of a lack of females and minorities in public higher education. Voting can easily take place along similar lines unconsciously premised on prejudicial micro-inequities.

INTRODUCTION

The tenure process is a closed system by definition, which contributes directly to coercion, groupthink, bias, and micro-inequities.

As Van Alstyne makes point of in his book, *Freedom and Tenure in the Academy*:

> The observation offered in this critique is that the installation, promotion, and tenuring of only those satisfying only such criteria as characterize the incumbent faculty's judgments – of what counts as "relevant" work and what counts in being a "competent" candidate – make the system self-sealing (literally self-proving of its own criteria) [inward looking and potentially discriminatory]. The incumbent faculty was itself selected and advanced by prevailing notions of "relevance" of subject matter interest and prevailing notions of "competence" to do suitable work. **Accordingly, succeeding generation of faculty may tend to be quite indistinguishable from the last generation. The structure of the system itself thus makes it more or less impervious to change** (IX).

Once voted into this elite group, with guaranteed lifetime employment, there is little chance of being voted out. If it is determined by a department head, school chair or senior administrator to take steps to terminate a faculty member for violation of state or federal laws, ethics or morality, a very lengthy process is initiated by the administration through the faculty affairs committee of the university senate to terminate the faculty member. This is where another obvious flaw exists. The faculty affairs committee, which oversees the termination of one of its own, is made up entirely of faculty who have tenure as well as the accused.

Ask yourself, who among the faculty senate would have an incentive to find cause to dismiss one of their own? The answer is nobody. Why would any faculty member of an oversight committee choose to set a precedent to get rid of one of their own? You can obviously see the problem in this process. Contrarians to this perspective would argue other professions have similar rules of expulsion; e.g. doctors and lawyers. Perhaps, not to be demeaning, but faculty with doctorates in psychology, education, engineering, music and many more, are not doctors or lawyers! The liability assumed by doctors and lawyers are mountains compared to the molehills of potential liability which non-professional doctorates possess.

To this end, equally embarrassing, and something that angered many of President Asher's advocates, was the manner in which the new president was welcomed into Probity University. President Asher came to Probity from being the Governor of his state. He has a degree from Harvard University and a law degree from Yale University. Not to be disrespectful to my faculty colleagues, but President Asher has greater credentials than most every faculty member I've ever met. Yet, when he was ready to take office, there were

INTRODUCTION

those misguided faculty members who protested his nomination; chanting he wasn't an academic. To this, it's easy to suggest that academics clearly aren't versed in basic business practices, or higher education wouldn't be where it is today.

It should be noted that the focus of this book is strictly limited to public institutions of higher education. Some will ask, "Why not private institutions of higher education?" The answer resides in taxpayer contributions.

Public institutions are partially funded by the taxpayers. These are the same individuals who suffer through our many recessions, borrow against their retirements and homes to put their children through college, and have now been forced to work past normal retirement age. Inflated college costs having the greatest impact on our country's wellbeing are those of our public institutions of higher education, and are therefore the target of this book.

As a public institution, we have a moral and ethical responsibility to be good stewards of taxpayer dollars and student tuition.

The original reason for tenure was academic freedom; however, studies have found that once a faculty member obtains tenure, their production (scholarship and research) begins to subside. In a recently quoted study, tenured faculty listed not wanting to have to find employment in mid-life as the number one reason for seeking tenure. Note that the original reason for tenure, academic freedom, was not listed as number one.

Personally, I would love to have guaranteed lifetime employment! Who among us wouldn't? I bet if I were to ask, in any one of our large lecture halls by show of hands, who would like to have guaranteed lifetime employment, every one of the four hundred plus students would raise their hand. Who wouldn't?

Add to that choice the almost impossibility of being fired. Think about it: no matter what I did, short of breaking a federal law, I could not be fired. Firsthand experiences, as well as thousands of others documented in literature, demonstrate how typically unacceptable behaviors in any other environment are written off because of a tenure process which lacks accountability (Horowitz xv).

The subset of things discussed below has been both witnessed and reported firsthand and is well documented by numerous authors. As a tenured faculty member, I can:

- Not do what my supervisor asks me to do; so long as I keep my teaching schedule.
- Teach a maximum of four classes per semester: roughly twenty hours per week, of a class I've been teaching for over 25 years.
- Teach as few as one or even zero classes per semester if I can get funding through a grant.
- Demonstrate extremely unprofessional and immature behavior; well, because that's just the way I am.
- Say whatever I wish to whomever I wish; believing falsely academic freedom protects me, although it doesn't, but then again, seldom has it ever been challenged.

INTRODUCTION

- Be openly, or passive-aggressive to any proposal change for whatever reason (after all, administration can't change the name of the college, merge departments, create new programs or do anything that might create efficiencies, save the taxpayers money or provide for a higher quality and more applicable education without the faculty approval – seriously!) This is true unless, of course, administration is willing to make major structural and infrastructure changes at great personal and professional career risk.
- Make $100,000 plus, 10 percent to 14 percent additional in my 403b and have full benefits; all while doing any and/or all of the above.

You really can't make this stuff up. I, like many of you, am astounded by all of this. In my many years working in business and industry, I have never seen so much waste and abuse of taxpayer money and student tuition dollars, let alone unprofessional and immature behaviors.

So who would offer such an employment scenario? Answer: nobody except academia. Public higher education is the only place in the world where guaranteed lifetime employment for the working class still exists in the form of what we call "tenure". Even Japan, the last country to provide for such a luxury, stopped the practice of guaranteed lifetime employment in 2001.

If it is the case that no organization or country provides guaranteed lifetime employment, then how is it that public higher education still does? The answer in short, and we will expand on this later, is through ever-increasing student tuition and "free taxpayer money". Think about it; if money is free, we have no incentive to create efficiencies, reduce redundancies, minimize costs, or the like. So long as the money is free, existing practices are allowed to continue. It is only when money becomes tighter; when state or federal funding is reduced or student debt becomes a national issue that the finger pointing really begins.

The Winds of Change

As the saying generally goes; "The winds of change are blowing the sands of time through the pages of history". We are standing at the precipice of seismic shifts in national and international higher education and public institutions of higher education in particular. The U.S. economy is stuck in neutral since the last recession (Moody's 1), tuition prices are skyrocketing, student loan debt has surpassed $1 trillion, parents – who have leveraged their homes through equity loans and second mortgages – are losing faith in the value of education, state funding is dwindling, federal grants are shrinking, and donor dollars are smaller. *But, entrenched in the past, guaranteed lifetime employment is alive and well, contributing to change resistance and long-term financial indebtedness of our taxpayer-funded public institutions of higher education.* These are the times in which we live. Change is inevitable. We can continue to do what we do until such time as we can't. Then we must do something else. This is the prevalence of the literature today; something has to give, something other than addressing the low hanging fruit of administrative cuts. The changes have to be institutional and must involve infrastructure.

There is a growing trend toward college and university mergers. Marcus states "...it's a kind of private sector-style consolidation that is becoming increasingly common, not only for public institutions, but also for nonprofit, independent ones that can pool their resources and cut their costs in a time of falling budgets and demand for efficiencies in higher education..." Marcus goes on to state "...there have been few mergers of colleges and universities in the past... but the pace of such consolidations is picking up..." What is happening is a very natural next phase in the business lifecycle; costs are rising, the number of new freshman entering into college is flat, and colleges and universities are experiencing the financial implications of reduced revenue and increased costs (Marcus 2).

In the end, we cannot afford to protect something that does not have an economic right to exist. Market forces will prevail as they always do; free money through taxpayer's indebtedness and rising tuition does not last forever.

Moody's, in the "January Industry Outlook" report of 2013, was negative about the financial prospects of higher education. They highlighted the consolidation trend as one of the "bolder actions by university leaders" that can "foster operating efficiencies and reduce overhead costs amid declining state support" by centralizing such services as marketing, fundraising, purchasing, and information technology.

In the report "The Next Generation University" (Selingo 2), the nonpartisan, New America Foundation, stated that higher education must adopt business practices to improve efficiency. The authors of the report state "...in the business world, the prevailing philosophy has long been that efficiencies and savings can be achieved by getting bigger and building economies of scale... which is why companies grow or merge with competitors..."

"It's not an easy thing politically," said Richard Novak, Senior Vice President for Programs and Research at the Association of Governing Boards of Universities and Colleges, "...you certainly have academic departments that have on the surface the most to lose, and will be the most vocal critics. **And faculty, who have tenure and job security, are the most likely to be outspoken about it** (Marcus 2)." Marcus goes on to state, "Everybody is realizing that we're not going back to the way things used to be... change is coming – and you can either get on board or be left by the side of the road (3)."

States have been increasingly rolling back their financial support for higher education, leaving their public universities, which already educate eight-in-ten Americans, scrambling for cash at a time when students are trying to get in. This leads to the finger pointing of inefficiencies. That pointing finger is almost always aimed at the oft-quoted "bloated administration" and "overbuilding" across any given campus. Remedies to increasing efficiency and reducing costs suggest (Selingo xiii):

- Limiting the number of majors and tying those remaining to the needs of the local economy

INTRODUCTION

- Offering classes year round
- Offering distance hybrid courses

Other suggestions are generally aligned to standard business practices of:

- Simplifying organizational structures by decreasing layers of management
- Increasing the number of direct reports for any given supervisor
- Eliminating redundancies in service organizations such as information technology (IT), human resources (HR), finance, or marketing through centralization, and consolidating purchasing (Kiley 1):

Most recently, David Wessel in *The Wall Street Journal* (1) sited four ideas to fix higher education:

- Use a stick – "…the federal government could link an institution's student aid to its track record, essentially punishing schools whose graduates do poorly in the job market…"
- President Obama could offer extra money to those colleges wishing to "…test new approaches shortening a path to degree…"
- Transparency – "…the administration argues that the higher-ed market would work better if students knew more about the careers and wages of graduates of programs they're considering and families knew more about the likely return on their big investment."

- Lowering barriers to entry – old rules "including an archaic system of deciding what's a college for purposes of federal aid and what isn't, may be preventing innovation…"

There is no shortage of ideas on how to fix the growing concerns of higher education. Over twenty-five years of literature reveals hundreds of potential solutions. While these are specific recommendations for colleges and universities to follow most are really nothing more than basic practices in any business/industry looking to increase efficiencies and reduce costs.

One of the more exhaustive studies of what action should be taken to grow revenue and increase cost efficiency comes from Moody's Investor Service, "Industry Outlook", January 16, 2013. Moody's negative outlook for higher education culminates in the following:

> …in the coming years, all universities will need to fund growing financial aid budgets, increasing healthcare costs, and capital improvement necessary to maintain or build market position. There is also a growing risk that public universities will be forced to assume payment responsibility for post-employment benefits that their respective states have historically paid. In order to do so, administrations will have to focus on traditional cost containment and operating efficiency, as well as take on the bigger issue of **tenure** and the student service intensive residential experience (16)."

INTRODUCTION

Their recommendations for change include:

- Centralization and shared services: human resources, fundraising, marketing, financial services, and information technology.
- Consolidation: within public systems; shared leadership and mergers.
- Expense flexibility: increase use of adjuncts; reduced percent of tenured faculty; leasing space for satellites/expansion.
- New market outreach: continuing education and degree completion; non-traditional students.
- Online education: distance learning programs; hybrid classes; fully online degrees; MOOCs for credit.
- Partnerships/collaborations: purchasing cooperatives; dual enrollment; joint BA/MA degree programs.
- Programmatic review: elimination of small, underutilized programs.
- Space utilization: weekend, evening, summer courses; moving administrative functions off core campuses to administrative spaces.
- Tuition pricing strategies: recalibration of the number of credits covered by the standard full-time tuition with per-credit charges for additional coursework (16-17).

The greatest long-term changes are not the low-hanging fruit, but the structural changes that have lasting impact. Changes that are structural in nature, and the most readily available to create efficiencies and reduce costs are seldom mentioned, and if mentioned seldom acted upon. These changes include: *centralization of our many decentralized colleges, elimination of programs which fail the return on investment calculation, and most blatantly, tenure, to be read "guaranteed lifetime employment"*.

On January 18, 2013, President Asher's "Open Letter to the faculty and staff of Probity" makes explicit reference to higher education as we know it being poised for big change. He goes into great detail highlighting concerns for higher education according to many literary works.

These include:

College costs too much

- Administrative costs have run up the cost to students without enhancing the value of education
- Rigor has weakened
- The system lacks accountability
- Too many professors are spending too much time writing papers for each other with no real contribution to understanding or human knowledge
- The unique system of tenure promotes "the narrowest form of closed-mindedness and the worst repression of dissident ideas"
- Athletics is out of control as a priority of university attention

President Asher goes on to say, "...the operating model employed by Probity and most American universities is

INTRODUCTION

antiquated and soon to be displaced..." In response to these many concerns and criticisms, President Asher offers suggestions for collective thought and action. To name a few:

- Excellence – Probity is not its buildings, or even its wonderful past or traditions "...this would be a great university if it met in a tent." Probity is its faculty and students and what happens when brought together effectively.
- Affordability – "...every university community should embrace the shared responsibility to reexamine current practices and expenditures with a determination to keep its tuition and fees within the reach of every qualified student..."
- Shared governance – "...shared governance implies shared accountability. It is neither equitable nor workable to demand shared governing power but declare that cost control and substandard performance in any part of Probity is someone else's problem. We cannot improve low on-time completion rates and maximize student success if no one is willing to modify his schedule, workload, or method of teaching..."
- Common purpose – "...the widespread duplication of identical functions can work against the common goal we must have of affordability and liberating resources for new investments in faculty and facilities... many choices will necessitate a communitarian outlook that consciously places the interests of the overall university first..."

Time and again, President Asher's "Open Letter to the faculty and staff of Probity" makes reference to being good stewards, creating efficiencies, becoming more effective, reexamining current practices and expenditures, and addressing the duplication of support function services. These and many other references are indicative of areas for improvement and alignment to their current mission. President Asher's strong background in business affords him great understanding of the steps necessary for economic success.

Yet another reputable summary is offered by Cook (Cook 1):

> Tenure may be the most misunderstood legal concept in American higher education, or perhaps it is not misunderstood but rather interpreted differently according to individual inclinations. Many faculty members consider tenure as their protection against the administration; their legal claim to employment for life, allowing them the academic freedom to do or not do whatever they will.
>
> Administrators consider tenure as an insurmountable impediment to flexibility; the legal hindrance to removing dysfunctional faculty or altering workloads.
>
> Students and staff see tenure as an unjustifiable shield for inefficient and improper behavior that would not be tolerated from them.
>
> Boards of regents and trustees view tenure as an anachronism; an outmoded legal concept created

INTRODUCTION

by faculty to allow them to study and teach esoteric concepts unattached to real educational and civic needs, precluding meaningful fiscal efficiency and performance accountability.

Government officials and business leaders consider tenure an undeserved legal privilege bestowed on a group of employees who they see as having light workloads and excessive control over their work environments.

No other profession, except federal judgeships, awards tenure. Any legal concept with this vagueness of meaning cannot survive. Without a common meaning or purpose, tenure will erode and eventually will disappear. The survival of tenure is therefore dependent upon framing a common definition and clarifying its parameters.

Tenure was created to ensure only that employment could not be severed for a single impermissible reason - to punish a faculty member for his or her exercise of independent research or relevant classroom speech, no matter how controversial. It protected the exercise of academic freedom. Tenure ensured that some form of institutional due process, using a peer-review system, was available for adjudicating threatened job terminations, to guarantee such punishments were not applied to faculty members exercising their legitimate academic freedom.

The issue then is how to return tenure to its singular original purpose from what it has become in some cases, a sinecure for the lazy and incompetent.

The original tenure contract offered by institutional employers to its faculty was simple: "We will not terminate your employment for your good-faith exercise of academic freedom, and if you think we are firing you in violation of your exercise of academic freedom, we will afford you a fair, internal, due-process review of that claim." The advancement of tenure to a protected property interest under the 14th Amendment adds no more to this construct than originally framed. The courts have not expanded the protections of tenure beyond this simple contract, but institutions and faculty have gradually and persistently done so. Despite claims to the contrary, courts have not expanded tenure to protect a faculty member's job if his or her speech, inside and outside the classroom, is disruptive and unrelated to the subject matter he or she is assigned. Nor does tenure permit a faculty member to be abusive to colleagues or students, or even to administrators; nor does it protect the faculty member's job because he or she took internal personnel disputes outside of the university into the public arena. And tenure does not protect a faculty member's refusal of a legitimate teaching assignment or the refusal to fulfill a reasonable increase in teaching load. Nor does tenure allow a faculty member to submit a research grant the university does not want to accept, or guarantee space or resources indefinitely. Nor is a faculty member justified in doing unlimited outside work or in failing to disclose to the university inventions or other discoveries resulting from his or her research.

In 2012, the National Academies of Science produced a report titled "Research Universities and the Future of America: Ten Breakthrough Actions Vital to Nation's Prosperity and Security". In this report, Recommendation #4 focused entirely on increasing productivity and reducing inefficiencies, stating "...the nation's research universities should set and achieve bold goals in cost containment, efficiency and productivity in business operations and academic programs..." Changes relative to increasing efficiency and reducing costs are directly impacted by the level of cooperation and collaboration of the administration and tenured faculty.

Guaranteed lifetime employment runs counter to three indisputable and undeniable basic tenants of efficiency and cost containment: (1) it creates an unjustifiable and

unsustainable long-term financial commitment on the part of the college/university (45+ years), (2) it creates a sense of entitlement, which, premised on fear, runs counter to creating efficiencies and reducing costs, and (3) as a process, it is biased, prejudicial and widely recognized as inherently discriminatory.

The goal of this book is not to initiate contention attendant to guaranteed lifetime employment; that conflict is already out there. It is to open a national dialog where we can begin to address the unjustifiable manifestation of something long since made obsolete. Successful conflict resolution would suggest,

> ...conflict is an inevitable and useful part of life. It often leads to change and generates insight. Few injustices are addressed without serious conflict. In the form of business competition, conflict helps create prosperity. And it lies at the heart of the democratic process, where the best decisions result not from a superficial consensus but from exploring different points of view and searching for creative solutions... the challenge is not to eliminate conflict but to transform it. It is to change the way we deal with our differences – from destructive, adversarial battling to hard-headed, side-by-side problem-solving (Fisher xiii).

The discussion that follows is intended to be constructive in nature, in that it moves to address the fears of change more

INTRODUCTION

so than simply pointing out the negative manifestations of holding guaranteed lifetime employment. That said, however, it is imperative the negative behavioral ramifications of guaranteed lifetime employment be understood, especially as they pertain to transforming public institutions of higher education.

To create a positive approach to change from what follows, sections are presented at the end which address common themes referenced by those who wish to maintain guaranteed lifetime employment and the status quo; alternatives to the existing guaranteed lifetime employment academic model; and a process for reaching an accommodating consensus on how best to move forward to the betterment of the student, taxpayer, university and the nation – this through the mediation process.

A few words on bullying versus discrimination and the use of the terms going forward. Discrimination is fairly well defined and has been for many years. Bullying, on the other hand, while not a recent abusive behavior, is evolving in definition and understanding, being increasingly discussed, and, is part of our awareness heightening on a nearly weekly basis.

In a recent article by Wilkie (2016), "more than one quarter of U.S. workers say they have been bullied at work, and another 21 percent say they have witnessed such abusive conduct, including threats, intimidation, humiliation, work sabotage or verbal abuse…" While bullying may very well be based on prejudice and discrimination, it clearly stands out as an entity seemingly in and of itself.

Wilkie goes on to say "...workplace aggression is on a continuum that stands out with general unaccountability, moves into instability [and then] to conflict, to mild bullying, to daily bullying... the goal is to create a power imbalance that will force a person to leave or create even more conflict... bullying often occurs in workplace cultures where highly powerful people, or those with high profile jobs, work alongside those with lower status..."

Wilkie attributes bullying to disciplines where there is a predominance of intrinsic behavior; that being, fields that want to heal, help, teach or develop impressionable minds. Education was identified as the second largest discipline (field) where bullying occurs. Wilkie identifies bullying behavior as unacceptable behaviors such as:

- Constant and unfair criticism
- Excessive teasing
- Yelling, shouting or screaming
- Insults and behind the back putdowns
- Hostile glares and other intimidating gestures
- Malicious gossip
- Monopolizing supplies and other resources
- Aggressive emails or notes
- Overt threats, aggression or violence

The point Wilkie eludes to, but stops short of saying, is that bullying is predominant in higher education, because those who practice it, have nothing to lose. Those engaged in bullying behavior have power by virtue of guaranteed lifetime employment (tenure) and cannot be fired or terminated because of their seemingly unprofessional or immature behaviors. Wilkie is correct in that higher education is flooded with bullying time and again. The literature, as well as first-hand experience supports this allegation.

This book does not explicitly call out bullying, but instead makes reference to a time tested, proven and openly acknowledged ill, that being inherent discrimination. Not explicitly referencing bullying by name, however, should not be construed as condoning or making light of this most detrimental and potentially illegal behavior.

A Word of Intent before Proceeding

It is not the intent of what follows to be a sharp, knife-twisting assessment of those who hold tenure; indeed, many of my best friends hold tenure rank. In fact, I will go one step further and say many of my tenured faculty friends work as hard as or harder than many of those I have known in business and industry. As much as I would like this not to be taken as a personal attack, some will interpret it as that. This book is quite simply a discussion of naturally derived behaviors attendant to having guaranteed lifetime employment. *In its simplest form, it addresses why guaranteed lifetime employment works against a sense of urgency, why guaranteed lifetime employment is a financial commitment that is unsustainable, and why the process used to give someone guaranteed lifetime employment is biased, prejudicial, and widely recognized as inherently discriminatory.*

It is my contention we should be able to have an open and honest conversation about literally anything. Unfortunately, as much as we don't want something to be an emotional exchange, there is always the potential that it will become one. This topic is no different.

This manuscript was reviewed by a great many highly intelligent people in higher education; many faculty and staff, two deans and a past university president. The reviews were usually along the lines of "...this is right on...", "...it hits the nail on the head...", and "...home run...". Unfortunately, the topic is so sensitive that those who earn a living off of the concept can't have their name or organization's name associated with this manuscript. Nevertheless, nothing happens without opening a conversation; that is the intent of this book.

I have roughly thirty-five books on my shelves and hundreds of applicable articles, written by college/university presidents, past presidents, provosts, faculty, staff and others not related directly to higher education. These many works offer insight into others' perceptions of how to fix higher education. This book is simply my contribution to this body of knowledge. I wish someone else would have addressed this problem with the content of what follows, but they have not. Many have alluded to it, and some have even dedicated a paragraph or two to it, but no one has written an entire book pointing out this issue and attendant concerns. This book is written for all those who wish they too could be part of this discussion in an open and frank manner, but fear they cannot.

CHAPTER 1

Truth #1: Protecting What Does Not Have an Economic Right to Exist; 45+ Years of Unsustainable Liability

In an open forum President Asher made the statement "we may not be a business, but that doesn't mean we can't act like one."

At their very basic level then, how do businesses work? To answer this requires a discussion on competition for funding, why cash is king, why there are mergers and acquisitions, and the role of stakeholders.

Why are for-profit businesses in business? Is it to serve the greater good? In some cases – and perhaps to some degree – yes. But, more generally, for-profit businesses are in business to make money…period!

What keeps businesses in business? The answer is simple: demand for their products and/or services. This demand in turn produces…again, money.

Why do businesses right-size, down-size, create efficiencies of scale, cut back, de-layer, smart-size, redeploy, force-shape, reduce in force…and lay-off? The answer: because we demand it! You might ask. "Who demands it?" We do is the answer – you, me and every other individual who purchases goods and services from business and industry. In every instance where the above actions have taken place, the price of the organization's stock has gone up. Why, you might ask? The answer is because we, the shareholders, want the greatest return on our investments. Money not paid to salaries goes directly to the bottom-line. A great example of this is reflected in figure 1.1.

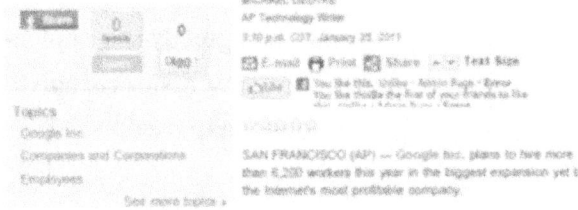

FIGURE 1.1

In 2011, Google announced plans to hire more than 6200 new employees. On the surface everyone applauded this. Even the President of the United States suggested how great this was for the economy and the many people of our great nation. I can't imagine anyone not being happy about this, especially given the then-state of the economy. But there were those not happy about the decision: the shareholders, as reflected in the above article.

Why wouldn't the shareholders be happy about the announced hiring like everyone else? The answer, according to the article, was quite simple; the proposed increase in salaries reduced the profits to the shareholders of the company. This seems preposterous on the surface. Who are these greedy shareholders so we might tar and feather them? The answer, surprisingly again, is us – you, me, and most every other taxpayer.

To fully appreciate the situation, we need further explanation. Consider the steps below:

- We work, and as a result, we make money.
- Given that we have extra available for a rainy day, we put our money in the investments with the highest returns; perhaps a savings account, or money market fund at our local lending institution, or wherever.
- The place you invest your rainy day funds has to compete with other institutions for your money; this to provide you with the greatest return on your money/ gain your investment.
- The institution you invest in has to find investments and make a profit, however small, for itself from your rainy day funds. To this end, your investment organization looks high and low for companies that produce the greatest returns to their investors.
- Companies which compete for this money have to create efficiencies to differentiate themselves from other companies wanting the same money from the same companies.
- To create the required efficiencies, these many companies yield higher profits by (drum roll please):

TRUTH #1: PROTECTING WHAT DOES NOT HAVE AN ECONOMIC...

outsourcing, reducing headcount, streamlining operations, and the like.
- In doing the above, these companies yield higher profits than their counterparts and gain investment company funds to allow these organizations to continue their operations.

In the end, the cycle begins with each of us wanting the greatest return for our hard-earned dollars. We, then, are the ones who demand efficiencies and cost frugality. We are the ones who demand right-sizing, down-sizing, creating efficiencies of scale, cutting back, de-layering, smart-sizing, redeploying, force-shaping, reduction in force...and laying-off. As the famous Walt Kelly was known to say, "We have met the enemy, and he is us."

An example of things happening which are not intuitively obvious as to why include the following:

On April 1, 2012, CBS News ran a segment. They were talking about Brevard County, Florida, the home of the space shuttle, from the Kennedy Space Center. In this segment, they discussed how the last shuttle launch was July 2011, after 50 years of liftoffs. On closing, Kennedy Space Center reduced heads by nearly 7,000. This in turn triggered another 7,000-person impact on the surrounding community because of mass business closings. The town was devastated by all of this. The question was why? Why did the Kennedy Space Center have to close? Why did so many Americans have to lose their jobs? The answer is not pretty, but is the essence of what drives businesses and allows them to stay in business;

money! The Kennedy Space Center closed to save $3 billion dollars a year in taxpayer money! They were quoted as saying "…it's not a personal thing; it's a financial thing…"

Why do mergers and acquisitions occur? Mergers and acquisitions are the coming together of two or more companies. But why? The answers are things we have already broached. Businesses merge to:

- create shareholder value
- create efficiencies
- target future markets with additional profitability
- serve combined markets more effectively
- reward stakeholders with higher returns

What does creating efficiencies and being more effective mean? Generally, in mergers and acquisitions it means reductions in plants, equipment, human capital, processes, and all the elements of efficiency gains.

One final question is: who are the stakeholders we've been referencing? Stakeholders are:

- shareholders who hold stock, options, and other financial instruments
- served populations; individuals, companies, states and Government
- employees; responsibility to local population, city and state
- competitors; who are occasionally our strategic partners in financial pursuits

TRUTH #1: PROTECTING WHAT DOES NOT HAVE AN ECONOMIC...

Accommodating our stakeholders frequently requires making decisions that benefit some at the expense of others. So in the end, we have to ask ourselves in every business decision, "What side do we take?" and "Whose interest will we serve?"

Given all of this, for-profit businesses are motivated to a large extent to stay in business, which requires money. The key to gaining money is quite simple, make more in terms of gross revenue, spend less in terms of expenses, or alternatively, return less to our rainy day account.

Why does this model not work to motivate academia? Because we – the taxpayers – allow public universities to stay in business by providing **free** money. It does not have to be earned. For state institutions, money is provided in terms of "general funds" because as a state and country, we support and value education. If we are anything, we are what we know. What we know stems from our educational system, which includes public higher education. *Free money, however, has afforded universities the luxury of supporting guaranteed lifetime employment with raises for time-in-position.* This level of entitlement as discussed above, promotes, a complacency which totally douses the flames of the burning platform. This therefore reduces the required call-to-action. Free money does nothing to instill the sense of urgency required to run an effective or efficient university, any more than it does a business or industry.

Not long ago, I talked to an assistant professor who was nearing her tenure vote. Her comments were straightforward. She said it wasn't the feeling of camaraderie she was looking for, or the right to freedom of speech – which she doesn't believe to be an issue in today's current environment – but that she could have guaranteed lifetime employment if voted in. She said it was the greatest "sham" imaginable, but she wanted into it if she could get it. She went on to say others have confided in her the tremendous sense of relief after having received tenure. *Knowing they would never have to look for work again was a major relief and de-stressor.*

The reality that a given business cannot be everything to everyone is another very important characteristic of companies wanting to stay in business. To remain competitive, a business must provide a good value for the customers' money. In business parley, this means having to focus on what they do best and not do what others do better. For example, gas stations predominately sell gas, and of recent provide limited grocery staples for those wishing milk and the like. Barbershops provide hair services; they do not sell automobiles. Even those in the defense industry, of which I was a part for many years, provide defense-related products and services; they do not sell ice cream or deliver mail packages. For a business to be successful, it must choose the specific markets in which it wishes to participate. No business can be everything to everybody and expect to stay in business.

This concept of selecting a market niche is equally applicable to public higher education. Within a state system of colleges and universities, it makes sense that some universities provide predominate types of courses and curriculum, while other universities provide other types. However; it is insensibly common for a university or college to provide a large breadth of programs including those in which it does not specialize.

By having such a broad offering, many universities dilute their financial resources and weaken their abilities to create or sustain the preeminence in their true areas of focus. In business and industry, this type of be-all-to-everyone is not financially feasible. Neither does it make sense for academic institutions which receive taxpayer funding and rely on continually escalating student tuition and fees.

If this makes sense to those reading it, then why would we not want to focus our resources to the best interest of the general public and ourselves as well? *Only a few seconds of thought would suggest that those with guaranteed lifetime employment might be opposed, but why? The answer is because if a program of study goes away, so too may the tenured faculty.* This is the only scenario where tenured faculty may be reduced from the workforce; only the shutdown of a given program can justify their dismissal. In reality, when a program is shut down, most of the potentially impacted faculty are given opportunities in other departments. These other departments, not wanting to set the precedent of reducing tenured faculty, generally find means to absorb those whose programs have been eliminated. Yet on the whole, programs very seldom go away.

In conversation with a friend from a peer institution, he said recently, his university performed an Academic Program Assessment where each program was evaluated for incoming freshmen enrollment and subsequent revenue versus the number of equivalent full-time, tenured faculty. The results of the study prompted a second round of questions to the colleges with these weak programs. They were asked how the harboring colleges intended to resolve this negative financial return on investment discrepancy. In one college, they had three separate programs in one department with one new student in one of the programs, two new students in the second program, and ten new students in the third for a total of thirteen new students in the combined three programs. Unfortunately, these thirteen new students had a total of fourteen faculty members. What a great deal for the students – more than one faculty member per student; what a really bad deal for the taxpayers and student tuition!

The head of these programs' housing department proposed a solution: create a single, core set of courses and make each of the troubled programs a concentration under the core. On the surface this sounds like a solution, but is it really? The weak programs did not change, nor did the number of faculty. The only thing that did change was how these three losing programs are now reported as one. The new program still has fourteen faculty members for thirteen students… nothing changed. Who, as an aside, were the biggest advocates of this new concept? As might be expected, it was the tenured faculty who understood the potential implication of their programs being shut down. This explains why so few programs are ever shut down and why there is such a proliferation of courses and curriculums.

Dickeson quips on this by saying "…if you believe in reincarnation, come back as an academic program and enjoy eternal life" (53).

In summary, we can't be everything to everybody. Even in public higher education, focus is a fundamental element of efficiency and effectiveness.

Recessions and Unemployment

There are no strict definitions of a "recession". Different groups define recessions differently based on varying economic, social, and political factors. The National Bureau of Economic Research (NBER) has been identified as the official organization relied on to determine the beginning and ending of a recession. The NBER is a private organization working to assist the public in understanding the U.S. economy; it is not an official government agency. A recession is typically declared based on a series of highly interrelated economic conditions. These conditions are generally related to consumer confidence, goods purchased, corporate hiring practices, unemployment claims, and investment and stock market valuations. Contractions or expansions in these and other criteria over a period of time are frequently seen as a marker of a recessionary period.

> The point where a recession begins is known as a peak. The point where a recession ends is known as a trough. Following the trough, the economy expands again towards another peak. Economist call the period of time between two peaks a business cycle (6).

In an expanding economic cycle, the business spiral is upward. The logic is as follows:

- Consumers feel confident in the current state of the economy – they feel they are safe in their jobs or other employment being readily available.
- Confidence in the economy fuels increased consumer buying.
- To meet the consumer demand, companies need to produce more products.
- To produce more products, companies buy more raw materials and ultimately hire more people, who in turn participate in the upward spiral through more buying.
- Investors see the increased production as a sign of a healthy organization and are more willing to invest in the company.
- In response to increases in stock purchases, the stock market goes up, pushing company stock prices upward in relation to stock-buyer supply and demand.
- The cycle continues as the market rises and more profits are made.

In a contracting economic cycle, the cycle reverses itself. The above steps are the same, but the effects are reversed. The hinge on direction is premised in consumer confidence. The downward spiral follows the following logic:

- Consumers do not feel confident about the economy – there is fear of losing their jobs or suffering through a period of unemployment causing potential financial hardship.
- A lack of confidence causes a slowing of purchasing.

- A slowdown in purchasing causes companies to slow production.
- Slower production slows the purchases of raw materials and slows hiring or, may cause layoffs.
- Fearing a company's growth is slowing, investors seek other havens for their investments, therefore reducing the amount of investment going into companies.
- As investors sit on the sidelines and do not invest or seek alternative places for their money, the stock market spirals downward producing overall lower returns on investments, again in relation to stock-buyer supply and demand.

Although these given scenarios are short descriptions, the general depiction and concept is historically solid.

While no one agrees to the number of total recessions in the U.S., the NYBERG suggests the existence of 32 U.S. economic recessions dating back to 1857. Others have suggested we have had forty-seven economic recessions dating back to 1790. Unfortunately, data recording methods and record maintenance have not been consistent. Consequently, naming an exact number of recessions is difficult.

According to the NBER, the average length of the 32 recorded recessions has been 16 months. NBER has reported the following average lengths for recessionary periods:

- 1854 – 1919 (16 cycles) – 22 months in duration
- 1919 – 1945 (6 cycles) – 18 months in duration
- 1945 – 2009 (11 cycles) – 11 months in duration

The two most recent recessions occurred from March 2001 to November 2001 and from December 2007 to June 2009. The latter period is the last recorded and declared recession in the U.S.

Economic downturns can be simply a function of economic cycles of contraction and expansion. They can also be something much more significant, such as a transition from one major socio-economic period to another. An example of the latter is when the U.S. economy transitioned from an agrarian economy to an industrial economy.

Looking first at regular economic expansions and contractions, there are two generally observed behaviors – employment implications and corporate efficiency gains. These two issues are discussed in the section, "How Business Works".

In the latter scenario, when a country transitions from one socio-economic period to the next, such as from an agrarian economy to an industrial economy, there is the potential for a major skills mix issue to develop. A skills mix can be readily identified when there is a substantial unemployment rate, yet there exists significant unfilled positions in the labor market. For example, at one point, industry was undergoing a reduction in personnel aligned to business shrinkage, while at the same time, there existed large numbers of unfilled positions. The issue was solely one of a skills mix issue. While hardware engineers of nearly all types in this organization were in over-supply, systems engineers were in very big demand.

Even in today's manufacturing environment, while we are producing roughly the same output of product, it is with one-third less manufacturing employees. At the same time, significant unfilled positions exist in the manufacturing markets. The skilled labor availability, or lack thereof, is further described below.

Oversupply of Tenured Professors in the Academy

We are hurrying to enhance the skills of our worldwide collective intelligence. The number of highly skilled candidates who can deliver required institutional instruction is growing and at an amazing pace. Additionally, those with greater capability, due to more recent and applicable skills training, are tremendously unemployed and/or underemployed.

While there may be a forecasted shortfall of skilled labor in business and industry, this is not the case in public institutions of higher education. The following example, using the most recent available data, suggests that roughly 236,250 people holding doctorate degrees are currently unemployed. By any definition, this is not a labor shortage on the whole for this group of individuals.

The United States Census Bureau conducts a Current Population Survey each month for the Bureau of Labor Statistics. The 2013 briefing titled "Recent College Graduates in the U.S. Labor Force" provides the most recent employment data for the 2011 cohort of graduating students.

This report provides the best estimate of college graduates and their post-graduation employment. The data is presented by race, gender, and degree type. The data reflects roughly 1.3 million people receiving college degrees; either bachelor's, master's or doctorate degrees. Of those 1.3 million people, 1.9 percent obtained doctorate degrees. These degrees are not to be confused with professional degrees. Professional degrees are typically categorized as medical, dental, law, and other related disciplines. This 1.9 percent represents roughly 65,000 individuals.

The Current Population Survey, Earnings and Unemployment Rates by Educational Attainment chart reflects an overall 2.5 percent unemployment rate for all individuals holding a doctorate degree. This 2.5 percent is of the entire U.S. population who hold doctorate degrees. The number of people in the United States who hold doctorate degrees is roughly 3 percent, which for purposes of this example we can snapshot from the World Population Clock at 315 million people. Therefore, 3 percent of 315 million citizens of the U.S. accounts for 9,450,000, of which 2.5 percent are unemployed. This data, then, suggests roughly 236,250 people holding doctorate degrees are unemployed as of this snapshot.

In 2011, it was estimated 236,250 people holding doctorate degrees were unemployed with another 65,000 graduating in this same year. According to the U.S. Bureau of Labor Statistics, in an October 2011 snapshot, 81.8 percent of college graduates age 20-29 held bachelor's degrees, 12.5 percent held master's degrees, 3.8 percent held professional degrees and 1.9 percent held doctoral degrees.

A doctorate is an academic degree of the highest level. There are three types of doctorates: research, professional, and honorary (Black 2).

The most common type of research doctorate is a Ph.D. (Philosophy Doctor or Doctor of Philosophy). In the U.S.A. the minimum time for completing a Ph.D. is usually 3 years following the completion of a master's degree. Although completions within this period are possible, most candidates take considerably longer: anywhere from five to seven years.

Professional doctoral degrees (also called first professional degrees) are awarded in certain fields where most holders of the degree are not engaged primarily in scholarly research and academic activities, but rather in a profession, such as law, medicine, music, or ministry. The minimum term for such a degree is typically three years.

Honorary doctorates are given when a university wishes to formally recognize an individual's contributions to a particular field or philanthropic efforts.

Below lists just a few of the many identified research doctorates:

- Doctor of Arts (D.A.)
- Doctor of Architecture (D.Arch.)
- Doctor of Applied Science (D.A.S.)
- Doctor of Business Administration (D.B.A.)
- Doctor of Chemistry (D.Chem.)

- Doctor of Criminal Justice (D.C.J.)
- Doctor of Comparative/Civil Law (D.C.L.)
- Doctor of Criminology (D.Crim.)
- Doctor of Environmental Design (D.E.D.)
- Doctor of Engineering (D.Eng.)
- Doctor of Environment (D.Env.)
- Doctor of Engineering Science (D.E.Sc./Sc.D.E.)
- Doctor of Forestry (D.F.)
- Doctor of Fine Arts (D.F.A.)
- Doctor of Geological Science (D.G.S.)
- Doctor of Hebrew Literature/Letters (D.H.L.)
- Doctor of Health and Safety (D.H.S.)
- Doctor of Hebrew Studies (D.H.S.)
- Doctor of Industrial Technology (D.I.T.)
- Doctor of Library Science (D.L.S.)
- Doctor of Music (D.M.)
- Doctor of Musical Arts (D.M.A.)
- Doctor of Musical Education (D.M.E.)
- Doctor of Ministry (D.Min./D.M.)
- Doctor of Modern Languages (D.M.L.)
- Doctor of Music Ministry (D.M.M.)
- Doctor of Medical Science (D.M.Sc.)
- Doctor of Nursing Science (D.N.Sc.)
- Doctor of Public Administration (D.P.H.)
- Doctor of Physical Education (D.P.E.)
- Doctor of Public Health (D.P.H.)
- Doctor of Professional Studies (D.P.S.)
- Doctor of Design (Dr.DES)
- Doctor of Religious Education (D.R.E.)
- Doctor of Recreation (D.Rec./D.R.)

- Doctor of Science (D.Sc./Sc.D.)
- Doctor of Science in Dentistry (D.Sc.D.)
- Doctor of Science and Hygiene (D.Sc.H.)
- Doctor of Science in Veterinary Medicine (D.Sc.V.M.)
- Doctor of Sacred Music (D.S.M.)
- Doctor of Social Science (D.S.Sc.)
- Doctor of Social Work (D.S.W.)
- Doctor of Education (Ed.D.)
- Doctor of Canon Law (J.C.D.)
- Doctor of Juristic Science (J.S.D.)
- Doctor of the Science of Law (L.Sc.D.)
- Doctor of Rehabilitation (Rh.D.)
- Doctor of Juridical Science (S.J.D.)
- Doctor of Sacred Theology (S.T.D.)
- Doctor of Theology (Th.D.)

Professional Doctorates are typically categorized as:

- D.C. (Doctor of Chiropractic)
- D.D.S. (Doctor of Dental Surgery)
- J.D. (Juris Doctor or Doctor of Law)
- M.D. (Medicinae Doctor or Doctor of Medicine) (US)
- D.P.T. (Doctor of Physical Therapy)
- D.O. (Doctor of Osteopathic Medicine)
- D.P.M. (Doctor of Podiatric Medicine)
- D.M.D. (Doctor of Dental Medicine)
- D.V.M. (Doctor of Veterinary Medicine)
- Psy.D. (Doctor of Psychology)
- Pharm.D. (Doctor of Pharmacy)
- O.D. (Optometry Doctor or Doctor of Optometry)

In a recent article (PBS News Hour 1), there was an interesting investigation into the graying of the academic professoriate. Numerous faculty members were interviewed on their current chronological age and their remaining in the workforce. In the article, Judy Woodruff talked to professors who were aged 65 and above, including a few aged 75 and above with the oldest being 80 years of age. In each of these instances the fully tenured professors were asked when they thought they might retire. Their answer, nearly unanimously was "...never..."

The article points out seventy-five percent of the tenured faculty in academia plan to work well past the normal retirement age. This is evidenced by the number of 65 and above aged faculty members having nearly doubled since 2000. At present, nearly forty percent say they will work past 65 years of age. "And why not?" suggests one tenured professor. "The work isn't demanding and the pay is great." Most all interviewed suggested they want to continue to do something in retirement and this might as well be it. To quote one of the professors interviewed "...most of us believe we should be able to work on our own terms for as long as we want..."

The problem with this cancerous mindset, of course, is the overwhelming supply of younger PhD graduates who are technologically savvy and not able to find work in the professoriate. As an eighty year old tenured professor stated "...older scholars are clogging the pipeline for the younger ones. The number of PhDs now far outstrips the number of tenured job openings..."

Mark Bauerlein, professor of English at Emory University, in an article for Bloomberg News titled *Old Professors Never Quit, They Just Hang Around*, wrote an assessment piece describing the impact of the rising cost of tuition on institutions of higher education and the impediments to transformation caused by tenure. He writes:

> Millions of 18 year olds are excited about heading to college this month... however they may be startled to find that the professor who enters Calculus I or Intro to Philosophy is more than a half-century older than they are. The phenomenon of the teacher who sticks around well past age 70 has been widely noted, yet colleges have had little success in mitigating its impact. **In today's economy, is there any worse policy than guaranteeing an employee the same job for 40-plus years?**
>
> That's what tenure ensures. An assistant professor comes up for promotion at about age 35, and if the candidate qualifies, the school maintains him or her until the professor (or death) decides otherwise. Granting tenure in 2010 commits the school to that employee until 2050 or beyond.
>
> The school not only has no flexibility to shift the workforce when demand goes down – a professor of sociology can't shift to chemistry – but also

has to pay a higher cost for the employee every year (because of ordinary salary adjustments, pension contributions and medical coverage).

Obviously, some of these professors aren't needed now. But ever since 1994, when mandatory retirement rules were ended, administrators can't make them leave. The only way to force a tenured professor out is to close an entire department, a step few schools have taken.

Tenure started 100 years ago as a way to preserve academic freedom, not to keep employees in place 10 years past customary retirement age. The continued resistance to reform shows arrogant disregard for rising college costs for students, for meritocratic decision-making and for academic innovation (1).

Generally speaking, for most all human beings, the negative effect of chronological aging on cognitive function begins to show signs in our 50's with significantly greater decline by age 70. Aside from these many physical, mental, and psychological breakdowns, senior tenured faculty are disconnected from newer technology required by today's college students. The concept of Facebook, tweeting, and the use of LinkedIn are foreign. This ignores the digital nature of newer students and the lack of technological savvy needed for distance-based program delivery. Standing behind a blackboard using chalk is a total disconnect from today's college age students, and in fact should be considered a moral crime against the student learner. Likewise, using the old style cellophane transparencies is equally anti-technology based; yet they are still used.

The article points out that universities are trying to find creative ways to deal with these senior-aged, tenured, faculty members. A full one-third of George Mason's senior, tenured faculty are 60-plus years of age according to the PBS article (2).

When discussing non-tenured adjunct faculty, a recent article by Scott Jaschik writes on a study released by the National Bureau of Economic Research which reports new students learn more when their instructors are adjuncts than when they are tenure-track professors (1). The author stops short of speculating on the many potential reasons for this.

In 2000, Jack Welch, Chairman of the Board and Chief Executive Officer of GE, changed history and subsequently changed the course for the way business and industry deals with reductions in force. In the opening letter to the shareholders, Welch states:

> In every evaluation and reward system, we break our population down into three categories: the top 20%, the high-performance middle 70% and the bottom 10%.
>
> The top 20% must be loved, nurtured, and rewarded in the soul and wallet because they are the ones who make magic happen. Losing one

of these people must be held up as a leadership sin – a real failing.

The top 20% and middle 70% are not permanent labels. People move between them all the time. However, the bottom 10%, in our experience, tends to remain there. A company that bets its future on its people must remove that lower 10%, and keep removing it every year – always raising the bar of performance and increasing the quality of its leadership.

Not removing that bottom 10% early in their careers is not only a management failure, but false kindness as well – a form of cruelty – because inevitably a new leader will come into a business and take out that bottom 10% right away, leaving them – sometimes midway through a career – stranded and having to start over somewhere else.

Removing marginal performers early in their careers is doing the right thing for them; leaving them in place to settle into a career that will inevitably be terminated is not. GE leaders must not only understand the necessity to encourage, inspire, and reward that top 20%, and be sure that the high-performance 70% is always energized to improve and move upward, they must develop the determination

TRUTH #1: PROTECTING WHAT DOES NOT HAVE AN ECONOMIC...

to change out, always humanely, that bottom 10%, and do it every year. That is how real meritocracies are created and thrive.

What Jack Welch and his senior leadership team did was to open the door to making personnel rotation culturally acceptable. In other words, layoffs of the bottom ten percent were not only an acceptable behavior in corporations, but an expected behavior if the organization wished to be competitive in a growing world marketplace. Further, his opening letter not only justified the rotation of personnel, but made it a "sin" and "failing" of management not to do so. His arguments made sense and even today this basic philosophy is employed throughout business and industry.

So, one has to ask, "Why wouldn't this same logic apply to institutions of higher education?" Certainly we all know of those who really should have been given the favor of an early out so they too might have started a more meaningful and fulfilling career earlier in life. Yet, today they hang on, feeling inferior, perhaps angry at their calling in life in the word of academics; yet, these individuals know they have no choice but to come to work every day and teach. The compounding "sin" is that our youth, whose minds are being formed for all of our futures, are being subjected to these less than enthusiastic teachers. Why? Because of guaranteed lifetime employment. These individuals, who should have been rotated out decades ago, simply exist in place because they can. Worse, to repeat a theme, they're existing in place with a guaranteed salary, increases for time-in-position, working roughly twenty hours per week. On top of this, they are simply plowing through, or worse – hating their lives and jobs. Does this sound like the type of person we want teaching our children? They certainly exist and we've all met them.

Using the basic tenants of personnel rotation has proven most successful in those companies who exude preeminence. These companies are the ones who reside at the top of their peer lists; the top 500 U.S. firms, top 100 U.S. Technology firms, top 100 global firms, and the list goes on.

Who are Today's College Students

To better understand the best methods and educators to teach today's college student, the personality and challenges of the student needs to be considered.

The premise for this section is best described by an excellent, recently published book titled, *Generation on a Tightrope* by Levine & Dean In it, the authors present a snapshot of undergraduate students enrolled between 2009 and 2014. The book begins by laying the foundation:

> Today's college students are struggling to maintain their balance as they attempt to cross the gulf between their dreams and the diminished realities of the world in which they live. They are seeking security but live in an age of profound and unceasing change.
>
> They desperately want the economic opportunity their parents enjoyed, but are coming of

age during a deep recession with reduced career prospects. They want to believe in the American Dream and are optimistic about their personal futures, but they are pessimistic about the future of the country. They want to be autonomous grown-ups, but seem more dependent on their parents and the adults around them than any modern generation. They want intimacy – a partner and a family – but they are isolated, weak in face-to-face communication skills and live in a hook-up culture. They want to play by the rules, but they don't know the rules and the rules are in flux because of the dramatic changes in our economy, the rise of new technologies, the condition of our public and private institutions, and a world growing flatter. They want to live in an Internet World, a digitally connected globe, but the adults and social institutions around them are analog or digital immigrants, including their blackboard universities (ix).

Studying the labels given to this generation can be insightful as to their unique foundations. Levin and Dean nicely summarize the historical and current names being applied.

Current undergraduates have been called Millennials (Howe & Strauss, 1992) and generation 2K (Zoba, 1999) because they are a part of the first college generation of the twenty-first century. They have also been called generation Y (Tulgan, 2009) and generation iY (Elmore & Cathy, 2010), which is logical because they followed generation X and are partial to the Internet. There is generation Z (Hopkins, 2005) because they are the children of generation X. Building on that Internet theme are the meat and potatoes Internet generation (Milner, 2010), the too-easy-to-confuse-with-basketball net generation (Tapscott, 2008), the insightful digital natives (Palfrey & Gasser, 2010) and the less committal digital generation (Jukes, 2010). There must be an iGeneration somewhere but we haven't found it. Taking an entirely different tack are the names me-first generation (Lipkin, 2009), meaning they are a tad self-involved, and echo-boom generation (Alch, 2000), referring to the fact that these are the children of the baby boomers, not booming like their parents, just echoing, and so it goes.

As of this writing Millennials lead the pack in popularity with generation Y following second but seeming to have faded because it may or may not refer to a somewhat older group of young people (5).

Two of the many characteristics of this study are the digital nature of this most recent cohort and the climate of continual change in which they live.

Colleges must educate this generation of undergraduates to thrive in an era of continuing change, to live productive and successful lives. "*A majority of undergraduates said their courses would be improved if they made greater use of technology, if their professors knew more about how to use technology, and if more of their classes made use of blended instruction, combining online and in-person classes (165).*" The parallel to this statement resides in this truth. How many of us know a grandparent or parent that doesn't know how to use Facebook or how to tweet, or even how to text on our smartphones? Think, then, how senior tenured faculty fit into this scenario. The parallel is unmistakable; the disconnect with today's students should be obvious.

> The Millennials, or digital natives as they are called, live in an anytime and anyplace world, operating twenty-four hours a day, seven days a week, unbounded by physical location. This causes a divergence between higher education and digital natives on the goals of education. Universities focus on teaching, the process of education, exposing students to instruction for specific lengths of time, whereas digital natives are more concerned with the outcomes of education, learning, and the mastery of content in the manner of games (166).
>
> Higher education and digital natives also favor different methods and models of instruction. This is reflected in a difference between

professors and students who approach knowledge in very different ways. Faculty members may be described as hunters who search for and generate knowledge to answer their questions. Digital natives by contrast are gatherers, who wade through a sea of data available to them in the disciplines, focusing on breadth versus depth of knowledge.

Digital natives are oriented more toward group learning and social networking, characterized by collaboration and sharing of content. This causes an ethical challenge for universities, which under certain circumstances view collaboration as cheating, and uncited content sharing as plagiarism (167).

Higher education is a provider driven in belief and practice. That is, the university, through its faculty, determines the curriculum, the content, the instructional methods, the study materials, and the class schedule. Digital natives tend to be consumer driven, preferring to choose if not the curriculum and content they wish to study, then the instructional method by which they learn best, the materials they use to learn, and the schedule by which they choose to study (167).

This is not the first time colleges and their students have been out of step. In the early nineteenth century as the industrial revolution mounted, "colleges in the main clung stubbornly to their classical curriculums, rooted in the ancient trivium and quadrivium and outmoded methods of instruction (167)." In the current era, we will not see higher education enrollments drop because college is now essential for obtaining most well-paying jobs. In fact, there are many positions in retail and services where once a high school education was sufficient that now require a bachelor's degree of one form or another. The old high school education as an entry into service management has now been upgraded to something beyond high school.

> The bachelor's degree, the symbol of success and the ticket to the middle class for the post-World War II generations, has slowly become the new high-school diploma. The number of people with college degrees holding jobs has swelled, even in professions not requiring them. By 2008, more than one in five clerical and sales workers had a college degree. Ten percent of services workers had one, as did one in twenty laborers (Selingo 7)…the number of people with a master's degree is now about equal to those with at least a bachelor's degree in 1960. Just as the bachelor's degree has become the new high-school diploma, the master's degree is turning into the new bachelor's degree, and it's probably only a matter of time before the doctorate is the new master's degree. It's called credential creep or credential inflation (10)…
>
> Colleges and universities will experience increasing competition from the for-profit sector, which views higher education as an industry ripe

for remaking, much as health care has been. At the same time, we are witnessing a convergence of knowledge-producing-and- distributing organizations that are entering the higher education marketplace: museums, libraries, media companies, software and game makers, zoos, and symphony orchestras, to name just a few (168).

So colleges must change because of increasing competition, but even more so because their students need a different brand of education. The purpose of the university has not changed. They remain for the preservation and advancement of knowledge and the education of our students for humane, productive, and satisfying lives. The activities of universities will continue to be teaching, research, and service. What must change, however, is the means by which we educate the digital natives who are and will be sitting in our classrooms. We must shift to employing varying calendars, locations, pedagogies, and learning materials consistent with the ways our students learn most effectively. It means that the curriculum must meet our students where they are, not where we hope they might be or where we are (169).

It doesn't make sense to tie education to a common process. Rooting education in a uniform amount of seat time, being exposed to teaching and a fixed clock, is outdated and no longer makes sense. The library must move from the periphery of college campus to its center. It has to be transformed from a storehouse for content to the central campus authority on knowledge; the discovery, incubation, distribution, application, combination and recombination of knowledge (170).

In an information economy, there is no more important social institution than the university in its capacity to fuel our economy, our society, and our minds. Every college and university needs to decide where it will stand on the digital spectrum. Will it be a brick institution (a college that focuses on campus life and close, face-to-face interaction between the members of the college community), a click institution (a university that offers instruction and services largely online), or a brick-and-click college, combining both (170)?

At the core of education for an information-based economy is an enriched version of the college major. We live in an interdisciplinary world that cannot be viewed adequately through the lens of a single discipline. The argument for disciplinary majors has been that they provide students with a deep body of knowledge and the skills to advance, question, and keep vital that body of knowledge. This remains essential today, but it is no longer sufficient.

Students need a broader, more interdisciplinary view of the world. Consider the following scenario: The enriched major might begin with an interdisciplinary class bringing together students of different majors led by faculty members from different disciplines focusing on a single problem. The conclusion might be a senior year course with a similar design, but in which the students are responsible for solving the problem (177). The question again becomes, does this sound like the type of change we would expect of senior tenured faculty or the type of innovation found in their younger counterparts?

I recently attended a conference for the North Central Association of the Higher Learning Council. One of the speakers was Dr. Mark Taylor, who is an extraordinary speaker. He has lectured and written on the teaching and learning of Generation NeXt for many years. In his presentation, he does an amazing job of summarizing the current college-aged, generational cohort; those under 26 years of age.

Dr. Taylor discusses this current generation as being very well managed – more likely over-managed. He introduces a model that transitions faculty in colleges and universities from the traditional teaching model to a more applicable model of learning. To emphasize this, he compares traditional teaching concepts to those typical of the newer learning model. These differences are reflected below:

Teaching needs to move from passive (teaching) to active (learning). By this, Dr. Taylor means we cannot continue to have students simply sit endlessly in one class after the next listening to lectures of talking heads. Unfortunately, this method is what the predominance of our current faculty are accustomed to and continue to employ.

We must move from students are who are disengaged (teaching) to engaged (learning). The approach Dr. Taylor used in his lecture of roughly 350 people was to use clickers. By asking questions and subsequently asking the session participants to click their responses, each was engaged in the discussion, not simply sitting while our talking head facilitator lectured to us. The clickers made for a much more engaging session.

We must move from being taught as students to taking responsibility for our learning. In this scenario, Dr. Taylor discusses an approach where talking-head lectures are recorded for student viewing before attending a class. Then when attending class, the student uses the time to apply the information from the lecture. In the least, this application of knowledge could be something similar to open discussion and delving the depths of our understanding.

In transitioning from content (teaching) to skills (learning), Dr. Taylor again cites the difference between going to class to learn content versus acquiring skills to demonstrate the application of knowledge. The above walks hand-in-hand with delivery of content (teaching) to discovery (learning). Discovery is more about the student learning through questions and exercises, or more generally, the application of assimilated knowledge. Discovery (through doing) has a longer-lasting impact than listening alone.

Besides observation and consideration, modern brain studies have revealed distinct differences in our comprehension levels depending on whether the learning or the doing model is chosen. Dr. Taylor's last teaching-to-learning transition moves from faith-based to evidence-based information. Evidence-based information is the underlying premise of Continuous Process Improvement (CPI) and the notion one can only make something better if it is measured. This is done by taking successive measurements and comparing them against an original baseline. This concept is well documented in what is termed "process management".

Process management relies on process definition, elimination of non-value-added activities, customer/supplier orientation, and a team approach (Hoban 44; Price 17). Process management processes utilize continuous process improvement (CPI), which assumes that a measurement baseline has been established. Through CPI, the process is measured forever. CPI accounts for error elimination, innovation, and business changes. All activities of a process are questioned; nothing is sacred.

Process management offers organizations of every type a means of applying the same quality improvement and defect-reduction techniques used in manufacturing processes. Many engineering, service, educational, and business processes offer an organization the greatest untapped potential for cost savings through quality and productivity improvement (Welsh 5). Process management, with its emphasis on business process quality, is the most meaningful way to apply the principle of quality throughout an enterprise (Zells 32).

The basic steps in creating an efficient process are:

- Determine what end result is desired.
- Identify the activities currently used to accomplish this process.
- Determine how the current activities are ordered (we call this the interrelatedness of the many activities).
- From the new flow chart created of activities and their ordering, ask which activities do not seem to add value, could be merged, or seem inappropriately placed in time.
- Create a new flow chart depicting the ideal scenario (don't worry about who currently does which activities or how).
- Identify measurement points in the new process that will allow you to determine how well the new process is working.
- Test the new process. In a business environment, this may mean making people assignments to the activities. It may further mean reassigning individuals or work in a manner not previously assigned.

As stated above, it is only through proper measurement that we can make required changes to an existing process in order to increase either efficiency or effectiveness. Proper measurement requires that we identify sufficient measurement points throughout our process, and that these measurement points are reflective of how the process is running. This is as applicable to academia as to business and industry.

Dwindling Enrollments

In Michigan, its colleges and universities are seeing the impact of dwindling enrollments. Kim Kozlowski (Kozlowski 1) reported "Michigan is producing fewer high school graduates". Central Michigan University reported an $18 million deficit in part because of a smaller incoming freshmen class and the shrinking pool of high school graduates, which is projected to continue for the next 15 years. Michigan, as suggested in the WICHE report, is home to the nation's second largest and fastest contraction of high school graduates, with only California projected to lose more and at a faster rate. Kozlowski reports:

> During the last decade, Michigan universities have struggled with revenue and boosted tuition after the state legislature slashed support to higher education when the economy faltered. Now the state's contraction of high school graduates has presented another challenge to universities, leading many schools to hustle for students beyond the traditional in-state applicant.

Declining student enrollments, as a result of declining high school graduates, is yet another contributing factor to the state of urgency in institutions of higher education. As stewards of public monies and student tuition, public institutions of higher education must address those unjustifiable costs (guaranteed lifetime employment) that prohibit the transformation of higher education for the betterment of all society.

Increasing Debt Loads

According to the Bureau of Economic Analysis, student debt has increased 511 percent since 2009.

In 2014, the average debt of a four year graduating student across public and private colleges and universities is $29,400. Student debt almost tripled between 2004 and 2012 and stands at over $1.3 trillion as of 2014: Q2 (Lee 9)

- 71% of 2012 students borrowed money
- 70% Increase in the number of borrowers
- 70% increase average balance per person

Primary reasons for growth in the number of borrowers and per-person debt load are two-fold: more people are attending college and more specifically, more people are attending graduate school.

The manifestation of this is: (a) parents are taking out school loans for their children, (b) students are staying longer in undergraduate programs and enrolling in greater numbers in graduate school, (c) loaning institutions are lowering repayment rates as borrowers delay payments through deferments and forbearances, and (d) discharging student debt is nearly impossible; the balance of the loan almost always stays with the borrower.

It seems logical to ask at this time "Why are college costs so high?" The responses to this question are plentiful. Literature is abundant suggesting college costs have soared because of the:

- proliferation of new construction on campus
- reduction in State funding
- increased number of administrators

- increased and excessive spending on sports, football fields and arenas
- quality and subsequent cost of food provided through our dormitories and comparable living quarters

Whatever the reason, and there is most likely a combination of reasons, **the one least mentioned is the most likely of all;** *the commitment to pay an individual for nearly fifty years into the future.* This commitment is made, not knowing whether this individual will be a good investment in 5, 10, or 15 years, let alone 50 years from now. Coupled with annual increases for time-in-position (i.e., just for being alive), this then poses a financial liability for the college or university that cannot be undone. Given that ninety-plus percent of a university's budget is labor, this scenario is unjustifiable.

What then are the implications of increasing student debt in a slowly growing job market? Generally speaking and significant to the economy, typical life-phase spending is being significantly altered:

Graduating seniors are moving back home instead of out on their own.

- Marriage and family are delayed.
- Purchases of material possessions which drive the economy (homes, cars, furniture, etc) are postponed.

Moving Back Home

Increasingly students, whether graduated or not, are moving back home. While there is no single authoritative source for actual percentages, a proliferation of studies reflect 34 percent of graduating students moved back home in 2011. A more recent survey reflected 60–85 percent of graduating students intended to move back home after graduation (Giang 1). This seems to be due to the slowly recovering economy from the last official recession – December 2007 through June 2009 – and a difficult job market.

CNN Money (Dickler 1) reported in 2011 that as many as 85 percent of graduating college seniors intended to move back home for at least a short while; this is up from 67 percent in 2006. PEW Research Center reported in December, 2011, that 53 percent had intended to move back home, at least for a short while.

Whatever data is used for reporting, clearly there is a trend that implies college graduates are in fact expecting to move back home, even if only for a short while after graduation.

Vivian Giang, reporting for *Business Insider* in 2012 states: "...It's becoming the norm for young people to move back in with their parents. In fact, 53 percent of 18-to-24 year olds are living with their parents and 85 percent of college seniors plan on moving back home after graduation" (Gang 1).

In March, 2012, PEW Research Center reported more generally,

> ...This generation of young adults has sometimes been labeled the 'boomerang generation' for its proclivity to move out of the family home for a time and then boomerang right back. The Great Recession seems to have accelerated this tendency. The Pew Research survey found that among all adults ages 18-34, twenty-four percent moved back in with their parents in recent years after living on their own because of economic conditions.

This same report reflected fifty-three percent of 18-24 year olds answered affirmatively to "percent saying they live with parents now or moved back in with parents temporarily because of economy." Forty-one percent agreed between the ages of 25-29 and seventeen percent agreed between the ages of 30-34.

February 9, 2012, PEW (4) reported

> ...More affluent adults and those with higher levels of education are among the most likely to say that young people are struggling in today's economy. Nearly half (48%) of college graduates say young adults are having the hardest time these days. This compares with 37% of those whose educational attainment is a high school diploma or less. Similarly, adults with annual household incomes of $75,000 or higher are much more likely than those making

less than that to say young people have been hit harder than their older counterparts (52% vs. 37%, respectively).

The PEW Research Center graphic (PEW 3) leads directly to subsequent discussion on the implications of the slowly recovering economy and difficult job market, the postponement of marriage and having children, and the purchasing of material possessions typical of age-specific cohorts. PEW in reporting on "How Economic Conditions Have Affected Young Adults' Lives", reported on the "percent of 18- to 34-year-olds saying they have done each in recent years because of economic conditions:"

- 49% – taken a job just to pay bills
- 35% – gone back to school
- 24% – taken an unpaid job
- 24% – moved back in with parents
- 22% – postponed having a baby
- 20% – postponed getting married

Postponing Marriage

From 1960 to 2010, the median age at first marriage went up nearly six years, from 22.8 years of age to 28.7 for males, and from 20.3 to 26.5 years of age for females (PEW 3).

In piecing together the puzzle, it is established that, due to rising costs and poor economic structure, college graduates are moving back home after graduation, and are postponing marriage in record numbers.

Aligned to the postponement of marriage are discussions on total fertility rate, education and fertility, income and fertility, and the biological implications of postponing having children.

The total fertility rate is premised on the number of babies the average woman would bear over the course of her life if she were to survive until the end of her reproductive years and age-specific birth rate were to remain constant.

> ...Demographers measure fertility in different ways. They start with the simplest observation: the number of births each year plotted against the numbers and ages of the rest of the population. From there they calculate the "crude birth rate," which is the number of children born per 1,000 people in that particular year. The crude birth rate isn't particularly useful, but for the sake of context, the U.S. population was about 312 million in 2011 and about 4 million babies were born, so the U.S. crude birth rate was around 13. By combining the crude birth rate with other census data, you can determine "completed fertility," which is the number of babies actually born to each woman in American by the time she's 50 and hanging up her spurs. And finally, there's the "total fertility rate." The TFR is closely related to completed fertility: It's the number of babies the average woman

would bear over the course of her life if she were to survive until the end of her reproductive years and age-specific birth rate were to remain constant (5).

A few quick facts on total fertility rate and its implications on the world population (Last 11).

- The American fertility rate currently sits at 1.93.
- In order for a country to maintain a steady population, it needs a fertility rate of 2.1.
- Due to the decreased birthrate of the Japanese and Italians (with fertility rates of about 1.4), they are on the verge of downsizing their countries. Their cities are dwindling; some small towns are on the cusp of simply closing.
- In 1979, the world's fertility rate was 6.0, today it's 2.52.

Relative to education and fertility, the more educated a woman becomes, the less children, on average, she has: (Last 12).

- U.S. average 1.93
- College graduate = 1.78
- Women with a graduate degree = 1.61

Education level	Total Fertility Rate
Not a high school graduate	2.447
High school, 4 years	1.947
College, 1 or more year	1.719
Associate's degree	1.820
Bachelor's degree	1.632
Graduate degree	1.596
Source: Jane Lawler Dye, U.S. Census Bureau, "Fertility of American Women: 2006," August 2008.	

FIGURE 1.2

Education, then, is directly correlated with delayed family formation. The drop in fertility among women with college and advanced degrees then, is in large part a function of delayed family formation.

Specifically, it's not just the length of education that diminishes fertility, or the careers the education makes possible, but the debt load the education incurs. Since 1987, when the Nellie Mae Corporation began keeping statistical track of student loans, the average student-loan burden on college graduates has almost quadrupled from $7,500 to $29,400.

In looking at income and fertility rates, there is again a direct correlation between increasingly higher levels of income and decreasing fertility rates. As the chart below depicts, a household income level under $20,000.00 represents the highest fertility rate at 2.038. As household income rises up through the range of roughly $75,000 to $100,000 per year, fertility rates decline and stabilize around 1.75 percent. Household incomes over $100,000 show a slight uptick from the 1.75 percent to 1.83 percent, but far less than the highest fertility rate of 2.038.

Household Income Level	Total Fertility Rate
Under $20,000	2.038
$20,000 to $29,000	1.988
$35,000 to $49,999	2.052
$50,000 to 74,999	1.734
$75,000 to $99,000	1.752
$100,000 and over	1.832
Source: Jane Lawler Dye, U.S. Census Bureau, "Fertility of American Women: 2006," August 2008.	

FIGURE 1.3

Given: young adult college graduates are assuming increasingly greater levels of school loan debt, are forced to move back home for a period of time, delay marriage in order to find gainful employment and establish their careers, all prior to having children. When, then, do these young individuals have their first-born child and how does that compare to previous generations?

The answer, as might be expected, is that the median age of first time parents has been skewed to the right; meaning the median age of first-time parents has gone up. Data reflects the median age for first-time parents has increased as much as 5 percent for mothers 30 to 35 years and older; this occurred while 20 to 30 year old first-time mothers simultaneously decreased in age by 3 percent.

In PEW Research Report titled "Recasting Motherhood 1990-2008", the Center for Disease Control depicted declining birth rates for three age categories: 15-19, 20-24, and 24-29; while depicting increasing birth rates for age groups 30-34, 35-39, and 40-44. In particular, birthrates for mothers whose ages were less than 20 declined by 3 percent, ages 20-34 declined by 3 percent, while mothers' whose ages were 35 and above increased by 5 percent.

From another perspective, the skewing of median age of first marriage and children has its limits. From a biological perspective, between the ages of 24 and 34, a woman's chance of becoming infertile increases from 3 percent to 8 percent. By 35, half of all women trying to get pregnant over the course of 8 months will not succeed. After 35, it gets even more difficult. By age 39, a woman has a 15 percent chance of being unable to conceive at all, and, by a woman's 43rd birthday, her chances of getting pregnant are nearly zero. All of which is why today, 1 out of every 100 babies born in the United States is created via in vitro fertilization (Last 51).

Postponing Material Purchases

As we chronologically age, we have very predictable patterns of spending. These patterns of spending are directly linked to what have been coined as gerontological life phases. When we refer to gerontological phases, we are referring to the scientific study of human development. This study is the science that seeks to understand how and why people change, and how and why they remain the same as they grow older (Berger & Thompson 4).

To help individuals better understand the developmental changes we experience as we grow older, there have been established three domains of human development: biosocial, cognitive, and psychosocial.

Biosocial development includes all of the growth and changes that occur in a person's body, the genetic, nutritional, and health factors that affect those developments, as well as motor skills – everything from grasping a rattle to driving a car. Social and cultural factors that affect these areas, such as duration of breastfeeding, education of children with special needs, attitudes about ideal body shape, and health habits that extend or shorten human life, are also part of biosocial development.

Cognitive development includes all the mental processes that are used to obtain knowledge or to become aware of the environment. It can include perception, imagination, judgment, memory, and language – the processes people use to think, decide, and learn. Education – including the formal curriculum within schools, informal tutoring by family and friends, and the results of individual curiosity and creativity – is also part of this domain.

Psychosocial development includes development of emotions, temperament, and social skills. The influences of family, friends, community, culture, and the larger society are particularly central to the psychosocial domain. Thus, cultural differences in the value afforded children, or in ideas about "appropriate" sex roles or what is regarded as the ideal family structure, are primarily explored in this domain (Berger & Thompson 5).

Gail Sheehy was one of the first to authoritatively document the basic consumption patterns of ageing individuals or cohorts. Harry Dent more recently aligned these patterns into actual accumulated date from the U.S. Bureau of Labor Statistics Consumer Expenditure Survey. Dent's findings can be summarized as follows.

- Single (ages 18 – 22)
- Young Married (ages 22 – 30)
  - Average age of first apartment: 26
- Young Family (ages 31 – 42)
  - Average age of 1st starter homes: 31
  - Average age of trade-up homes: 41
- Family, College Kids (ages 46 – 50)
  - Average age, largest consumption of furniture: 46
- Empty Nesters (ages 50+)
  - Average age for college tuition peak: 51
  - Average age for purchases of autos: 53
- Retired (60+)
  - Average age for hospital visits: 60
  - Average age vacation and retirement homes: 65
  - Average age for cruises: 70
  - Average age for predominance of prescription drugs: 77
  - Average age for nursing homes: 84

As we chronologically age, our life demands for shelter, transportation, food, and clothing all change. These many changes are a reflection in large part to our changing family makeup at distinct periods in time. From above, it can be construed that our U.S. populace generally get married in their 20's. The 30's are typically a time for the collection of material possessions (cars, homes, furniture, appliances, etc.) Our 40's reflect an empty nester's phase, where our children become, theoretically, independent and move out onto their own, whether this be college or simply moving away from home to begin working. During our 50's, we begin to notice the changes of primary ageing, that is, those changes related to biological changes in hearing, eye sight, and other physical changes that are frequently the underlying premise for sayings such as "...ageing is not for the faint of heart..."

The consumer life cycle presented above uses U.S. Census Bureau data to reflect the median age by which most Americans participate in a given event; for example, our first starter homes are purchased generally around the age of 31.

It becomes considerably more apparent when looking through the above lens to see the overall impact on our national economy that delaying adulthood can have. Skewing our purchases to the right places pressure on the entire economic infrastructure designed around historically predictable patterns of purchasing. In summary, delaying entry into adulthood, meaning moving away from home, being married, having children and all of the implications of this shift to the right, has a negative impact on the whole of the U.S.

Continuing this discussion is a significantly greater discussion on the aging of the population in the U.S. and the world as a whole. Just a few short points will shed sufficient light to gain an understanding of this other, most significant, piece of the puzzle.

In 1950, the median age in the U.S. was 30 years. In 2000 the median age had increased to 35. By 2050, the median age in the U.S. will be 40. As people age, they consume less in terms of material possessions. Those chronologically aged also reduce their earnings and subsequently their taxes, therefore reducing the overall U.S. tax base.

Complimenting this line of thinking is the required number of working adults 16-64 who pay into Social Security in support of those who draw down from this government-sponsored social support program. The ratio from 1940 (the first year social security checks were issued) to more recent 2010, declined from 159.4 workers supporting each retiree, to 2.9 workers supporting each retiree.

Ration of Workers Paying FICA Taxes to Retirees Collecting Social Security Benefits			
Year	Workers (in millions)	Beneficiaries (in millions)	Ratio (number of workers supporting each retiree)
1940	35.390	0.222	159.4
1950	48.2850	2.930	16.5
1960	72.530	14.262	5.1
1970	93.090	25.186	3.7
1980	113.656	35.118	3.2
1990	133.672	39.470	3.4
2000	155.295	45.166	3.4
2010	156.725	53.398	2.9
Source: Social Security administration (http://www.ssa.gov/history/ratios.html).			

FIGURE 1.4

The Social Security Administration predicts that by 2034, the ratio of workers-to-retirees will fall to just 2.1 workers for every retiree as a result of (1) roughly 809 million Baby Boomers retiring and (2) the declining fertility rates having failed to produce a proportionate number of new workers (Last 108).

Implications of our Understanding of this Generational Cohort

On the whole, we have a slowly recovering economy, difficult job market, high student debt, graduates moving back home after graduation, and delays in marriage, having children, and the purchasing of material possessions. All of this demands action for the betterment of our society and the world populous as a whole.

Although one could argue vehemently the root cause of any one of the above triggers of delayed adulthood, the perspective of this book suggests the precipice of change has to err on the side of continuing to educate our populous at a fair and reasonable cost. Initiatives at this point will bring student debt and all subsequent delays to the left of our ageing timeline.

This book provides evidence to suggest the solution to the underlying root cause of all these issues is cemented in lowering college costs. The premise of this discussion is based on cost reduction via the eradication of that which does not have an economic or any other right to exist, namely, guaranteed lifetime employment.

The Formation of Unions and their Purpose

The Industrial Revolution in the United States appears to have been the catalyst for the earliest forms of organizational design and management philosophies. Three advances in technology launched the period: the steam engine (1790–1810), the railroads (1830–50), and the telegraph (1844). These technologies are thought to have been responsible for the proliferation of U.S. entrepreneurship by 1860. Along with these technologies came increasing demand for manufactured goods and industrial markets. During the last half of the nineteenth century, the U.S. economy entered an explosive transition from an agricultural nation to an industrial nation.

With the transition into an industrial society came demand for more efficient and effective production techniques. The goal of this period was to meet demand. Quality and price frequently gave way to availability.

The Great Depression of 1929 saw unemployment in excess of 25 percent. Afterward, unions sought and gained major advantages for the working class. In this period, known as the golden age of unionism, legislatures and courts actively supported organized labor and the worker. In 1971, Graff and Krout described this event:

> The collapse of the stock market was the initial stage of the long and bleak great depression. Unemployment, which had been growing since the previous July, continued to increase at an alarming rate following the crash on Wall Street. Spending by consumers, which had been declining since July, continued to slacken. As businessmen stopped building new plants, the number of jobs available decreased.

Income was not distributed well enough to keep people employed through an increase in spending by consumers. Farmers found prices lower than ever; millions of working people could neither buy factory goods nor find employment. Middle-class people everywhere could not meet the time payments on their cars, refrigerators, or houses. The "prosperity decade" had ended with a sickening thud (631).

During these times of greater employee supply and lesser demand, employers easily solicited work from employees. During the industrialization period, quality and price frequently gave way to availability in production decisions. So too did employers sacrifice the human aspects of the work relationship during the lean years of the Depression. Added to this supply and demand imbalance were massive immigration numbers. Collectively, the industrialization period in U.S. socio-economic history, coupled with significant immigration, set the stage for the "golden age of unionism", as the value of individual workers decreased and replacement became more feasible.

Recognizing this problem, emphasis during this time shifted to attempts at understanding the needs of workers. The human-relations movement arose in the early 1930s. No activity better exemplifies this philosophy than the famous "Hawthorne studies" (1924–32) conducted by Harvard University psychologist Elton Mayo. The Hawthorne studies led to an increased interest in human problems in the workplace and a refocusing on the human factor of production.

Again, as was the case with the efforts of Frederick Taylor, many followed in Mayo's humanistic footsteps to better understand, describe, and document the intangible human relations of the time. One such person was Mary Parker Follett, who from 1920 to 1933, espoused a basic theory that the fundamental challenge for any organization was to build and maintain dynamic, yet harmonious, human relations within the organization. In 1938, Chester Barnard effectively integrated traditional management and the behavioral sciences. Barnard viewed the organization as a social structure and stressed the psychosocial aspects of organizations.

As long as there have been people making a living in one form or another, there has been the opportunity for labor issues; whether these are amount of money paid for work performed, hours of employment, workplace safety or a litany of other closely related work concerns.

To solve this problem of collective workplace concerns among employed individuals, unions came into existence. Unions were designed to provide a framework for the collective concerns of employees. The overall purpose of the union is to help individuals gain strength in numbers so there collective thoughts can be addressed by organizational senior bodies. Current union thrusts are focused toward increasing membership wages, therefore raising the standard of living of the working class, ensuring a safe working environment in which to perform the required work, and increasing benefits for workers and their families. All of this comes at a cost to be addressed in subsequent paragraphs. The perceived need for these collective voices stems from the basic business model described in the "How Business Works" section of this document. The focus of the organization is to remain financially competitive in an ever-changing, international environment, even at the perceived expense of its employees.

The Declining Need for Unionization

A very short history of unions reflects the formation of the American Federation of Labor (AFL) in 1886 and the Congress of Industrial Organizations (CIO) in 1935. The two merged in 1955. The percentage of workers belonging to a union in the U.S. peaked in 1954 at nearly 35 percent of the total population. Since that time, union membership has declined steadily to roughly 12 percent in 2013. The working population in unions transitioned from manufacturing and farming early on, to, and at present, being predominantly state and local government employment.

What was the reason for the decline in union representation? Keep in mind, the original purpose of the union concept was to increase wages, ensure a safe working environment, control-required hours of employment, and increase benefits. As we matured as a society, corporate policies, procedures, methodologies and practices, as well as state and federal legislation, created a declining need for union representation. This came as a result of most worker concerns being addressed in a positive and satisfactory manner through corporations, as well as state and federal laws.

Child labor was originally prohibited in 1949. Laws such as the Fair Labor Standards Act were designed to set labor standards for minimum wages, overtime pay, and child labor provisions. Title VII of the 1964 Civil Rights Act was amended by the 1972 Equal Employment Opportunity Act, barring discrimination based on numerous individual characteristics such as race, color, religion, sex, and national origin. The Privacy Act of 1974, applicable only to federal government agencies, provides federal government employees the right to view their own personnel files. The Fair Credit Reporting Act of 1971 requires an employer to notify job candidates of its intent to check into the potential employee's credit. The Drug Free Workplace Act of 1988 was passed to aid in keeping the problem of drugs from the workplace. Under this act, government related organizations must ensure a workplace that is drug free. There also exist numerous other federal acts including The Polygraph Protection Act of 1988, and The Worker Adjustment and Retraining Notification Act of 1988.

Point being, as indicated above, most every original concern of labor practice in the United States has in one form or another been adequately addressed and is no longer a concern, thus the predominant reason for the reduction in unionization. Add to this the negative perceptions and impact of unions on the economics of an organization, and one can readily understand the current dwindling membership and apathy from those not involved in a union.

Social Perspectives of Unionization

Unions have been under scrutiny for a number of years. The bailout of two of the larger automakers requiring $85 billion of taxpayer money was partly blamed on the high cost of unionization.

Others have pointed to the high cost of union salaries and benefits as the reason for needing to outsource. It is true, union wages are noticeably higher than nonunion worker wages. In 2012, the median weekly income of union workers was $943; this in comparison to nonunion workers' median weekly income of $742.

Approval of unions climbed during the 1980s, but declined below 50 percent by 2009. A Gallup poll released on March 9, 2012, reflected an overwhelming 49 percent of Americans were more likely to support limiting the collective bargaining powers of unions in order to balance a state's budget. The same poll reflected Americans were more likely (38 percent) than not (34 percent) to describe unions with a negative phrase versus a positive one. Another Gallup poll released on August 31, 2012, reflected a majority 42 percent of Americans want labor unions to have less influence. Americans 49 percent to 45 percent believe labor unions hurt the U.S. economy. And, 56 percent to 34 percent of Americans believe labor unions hurt workers who are not members of labor unions.

In the final analysis, the very reasons for unions to exist in the first place are losing validity. This lack of need has directly contributed to the dwindling union participation, and actually has placed unions in a negative social light. Citizen sentiment toward unions has turned to apathy at best and disdain at worst. Unions, in the United States, appear to no longer have an economic right to exist.

But wait – with this said, there is a renewed interest in unionizing adjunct faculty. This is in response to the mistreatment of adjuncts from tenured faculty as well as the attendant pay practices. This topic is addressed later.

Why Tenure Exists

Why does tenure exist? The origin of tenure can readily be traced back to the 1940 "Statement of Principles on Academic Freedom and Tenure." This joint declaration was an effort by professors and university/college presidents, endorsed by the Association of American Colleges (AAC).

The opening paragraphs of the 1940 statement lay the foundation for the primary purpose of the statement.

> Academic freedom is essential to these purposes and applies to both teaching and research. Freedom in research is fundamental to the advancement of truth. Academic freedom, in its teaching aspect, is fundamental for the protection of the rights of the teacher in teaching and of the student to freedom in learning....
>
> Tenure is a means to certain ends; specifically: (1) freedom of teaching and research and of extramural activities and (2) a sufficient degree of economic security to make the profession to men and women of ability. Freedom and economic security, hence tenure, are indispensable to the success of an institution in fulfilling its obligations to its students and to society. (1)

The Center for College Affordability and Productivity (CCAP 2), reflects on the origination of tenure stating:

The American Association of University Professors (AAUP) defined academic tenure in 1940 as:

"After the expiration of a probationary period, teachers or investigators should have permanent or continuous tenure, and their service should be terminated only for adequate cause, except in the case of retirement for age, or under extraordinary circumstances because of financial exigencies."

The concept of tenure in the United States dates back at least to 1915 when the American Association of University Professors (AAUP) established a declaration of academic freedom and tenure in response to a growing number of cases involving alleged infringement of academic freedom, as a means to protect academic freedom and to render the professorate "more attractive to men of high ability and strong personality". Upon receiving tenure, an employee may only be terminated for "adequate cause", unless an institution has "extraordinary circumstances because of financial exigencies" and thus, granting what one higher education researcher, Philo

Hutcheson, defined as "a contractual relationship, emphasizing the lifetime arrangement between an institution and a professor."

Education is one of the few industries in the United States that provides job tenure, which has drawn a steady flow of criticism over the past few decades as colleges have increasingly moved away from this employment arrangement (10-12).

Tenure then, by the above definition, is to protect those who need to do research and teach from those who might not like what the professors have to say on a given subject, or the manner in which the professors do or say what they feel is necessary to perform research or teaching.

What does this mean? As an example, if I am a professor who teaches math, science, or engineering, according to the statement above, it is possible I might say something in the classroom that appears contradictory to the college/university beliefs on the subject; so to this end, I need protection. Essentially, I should be allowed to say what I think best characterizes the subject matter. Math, science, and engineering don't seem to fit this scenario very well; perhaps studies in politics or religion serve as a better example. If this is true, then if I teach in such a manner on a religious perspective that conflicts with a hiring college/university, then I should be protected in an attempt to allow me, as the professor, to express my personal beliefs, albeit they may conflict with my employer.

Amacher points out "...if colleges actually stuck to the AAUP definition of a tenure, instead of to what tenure means in practice, it is unlikely that many people could find much to criticize about it" (11).

A number of individuals have asked the very basic question of why we have to protect academic freedom at all in today's environment. After all, we do have the constitution of the United States that provides for our basic freedom of speech. And more, how important is academic freedom to most of the professoriate anyway? Do we really need academic freedom to teach math or English, or psychology, or any number of other disciplines? What is so hard in today's environment to teach a given subject without creating such controversy as to require guaranteed lifetime employment?

Riley in "The Faculty Lounges" points out:

> ...if you count faculty in vocationally oriented departments, those who teach area, ethnic, cultural, and gender studies, as well as a significant chunk of the country's research scientists, you will arrive at a number that is more than half the tenured faculty in the United States...
>
> At the very least there is no reason why tenure shouldn't be abolished at the vast majority of the four-thousand degree-granting colleges and universities in the United States where academic freedom is an almost irrelevant

concept. When professors are engaged in imparting basic literacy skills, or even classes on how to cook or how to start a business, there is no reason why their academic freedom must be protected. At that point academic professors are just like any other employee. They have the right to speak freely, as guaranteed by the constitution, but they don't have the right to say whatever they want in their role at the university. And they don't have a right to a job regardless of what sort of nonsense they spout publically (41)...

For anyone in business and industry, this most likely seems point-on. If any individual in business or industry were to say something not representative of an organization's moral or philosophical perspective, certainly we would expect a call from Human Resources asking us to do our jobs and refrain from personal philosophizing. If I worked for Apple Computer and talked openly about how Apple products were not as good as other similar products, I should not be surprised if Apple Human Resources were to ask me to curtail my opinions, or alternatively perhaps, if I would feel more comfortable working for the other competing company.

The issue of tenure – guaranteed lifetime employment – most likely does not equally apply to all disciplines across a college or university table of offerings. In fact, remembering the conversation above on the growing intellectual capability of our world stage, my guess is that most all subjects, short of those very specialized niche subjects, can be backfilled with ready and willing professors possessing PhDs. In a different section, we offered evidence of a surplus of PhD-ready candidates who cannot find gainful employment because of senior tenured faculty who refuse to exit the workforce.

The 1940 statement and the awarding of tenure makes it essentially impossible to dismiss a professor for views expressed in the classroom, through scholarly writing, or in public forums. What, then, does constitute adequate cause for dismissal? There are three primary areas in which a fully tenured professor may be dismissed, only if proven and judged so by a committee of other tenured professors. These areas are (1) demonstrated incompetence or dishonesty in teaching or research, (2) substantial and manifest neglect of duty, and (3) personal conduct which substantially impairs the individual's fulfillment of his institutional responsibilities (Van Alstyne 328).

Van Alstyne, in his book titled *Freedom and Tenure in the Academy* offers:

> One can find a multiplicity of reasons for supposing that its [tenure] days are numbered. It has stepped on the toes of so many potential academic supporters; the libertarians who deplore its stand on freedom, the unionists who believe arbitration should be substituted for peer review, the many who expect more of it than it delivers and would wish it had said less on many counts, that one may wonder if

it will find another hereafter to befriend it. It is so out of touch with critical developments in the academic profession, such as the immense increase in the number of part-timers drawn from the casual labor market, and it is so out of sympathy with some of the current devices of academic management, such as non-tenure tracks and rolling short term contracts, that one may wonder whether the combination of a postmodern academic work force and a pre-modern administrative mentality will not finally do it in (328).

Riley, in her book *The Faculty Lounges*, recalls a panel discussion with representatives from the American Association of University Professors and the National Research Council where she was criticized for her stance on tenures ills. Riley recalls:

> ...On the one hand I was told that tenure was the best way to protect the right of professors to speak and write freely. On the other hand I was told that tenure was already on its way out, so there was no point in arguing about it... (4).

During the summer of 2010 the tenure issue began to heat up again. The New York Times conducted two on-line forums: "What if Tenure Dies?" and "The Professors Who Won't Retire." Slate's Christopher Beam wrote a piece called "Finishing School: The Case for Getting Rid of Tenure," and "Atlantic editor Megan McArdle wrote "Tenure, An Idea Whose Time Has Gone." Even some academics are getting back into it. September 2011 saw the publication of Mark Taylor's Crisis on Campus" (5).

Some have argued tenure does not necessarily mean guaranteed lifetime employment. Amacher (5) and others point out "…**in all cases the meaning is the same; the appointment is for life to the age of retirement**…"

College faculty focus on tenure because it is a quite natural human tendency to protect what one has. A natural question might be "Is it possible unionization will replace tenure on campuses throughout institutions of higher education?"

Riley addresses this; "…will things be worse if the tenure system is somehow replaced by mass unionization?" What is certain though is that more and more faculty members are fleeing into the arms of unions as the tenure system weakens. It's hard to blame adjuncts or even graduate students for thinking they need union protection, given their current work conditions. And, given the goals of big labor, it's easy to understand that these additional members will be warmly welcomed. All of which are good reasons to come up with a sensible alternative to both systems, one that offers reasonable salaries to talented people without the guarantee (through tenure or unions) of a job for life (117).

Why Tenure Fails the Taxpayer

There is a very significant cost to tenure. The most obvious cost is if the wrong people are granted tenure. In this instance the college/university can do essentially nothing to remove the ill-advised hire, so long as the professor does not violate one of the above basic tenants of guaranteed lifetime employment.

The second obvious cost of tenure is the long-term financial commitment on behalf of the employing institution. Assuming a professor is tenured within the seven years required to obtain said tenure, and begins his/her pursuit immediately after receiving his/her doctorate, that would make the newly employed tenured professor about 28 years of age. **If that newly tenured professor works until he/she wishes to no longer work (this because there is no mandatory retirement age); say for this example 70 years of age, that would mean the employing institution is making a 45+ year commitment to pay this individual a guaranteed salary plus annual increases for nothing more than time-in-position.** Meaning, if the professor does nothing more than the minimum required, and does not violate the above guidelines, he/she can stay gainfully employed for as long as they wish, and cannot be fired. From a financial perspective, multiply this thousands of times over, and it can be readily seen why some would suggest tenure not only does not have – but cannot have – an economic right to exist. **This type of financial model is unsustainable, especially if the burden of this cost is borne by the students and taxpayers who fund these many salaries.**

The Chronicle of Higher Education in 2013 conducted research of 1,251 U.S. colleges, and found that private institutions pay professors the highest salaries while also boasting the lowest ratio of students to faculty members than colleges in any other country globally (Kensing 3).

According to the Center for College Affordability and Productivity (CCAP 3):

> ...A major cost item for universities is the cost of instructors. **Costs for adjunct faculty are relatively low, but senior tenure-track faculty are very expensive**; at a few universities, salaries for full professors (including fringe benefits) rise to as high as an average of $200,000 annually. A large portion of faculty receive tenure, the equivalent of a lifetime employment contract. A decision to award tenure often means making a financial commitment with a discounted present value of two million dollars or more. Hardly any other occupation offers such an extraordinary employment arrangement. ...there are many objections to tenure. First, tenure is a costly way to achieve job security. Many superstar professors are not the slightest bit worried about job security (seeing as they get job offers all the time), and the abolition of tenure would not have much impact on their willingness to work. Tenure is most often prized by the least productive faculty—the ones

who would not receive an offer from another employer if they lost their current jobs. Tenure protects people who become incompetent or ineffective because of changing circumstances. It makes it difficult to reallocate resources over time as academic needs change. The natural inertia of faculty is fortified by tenure since they have little to lose in opposing cost-saving or service enhancing measures (10).

Many have argued tenured professors accept low wages in exchange for their lifetime appointment in the academy (Amacher & Meiners 3). It can be readily seen this is no longer true. Many highly educated holders of doctorate degrees would like to earn the average salaries of faculty professors. The below discussion addresses salaries at some of the public and private institutions in the United States. In 2013, The Chronicle of Higher Education surveyed roughly 1250 institutions of higher education. Their complete findings by institution may be found on their website.

If a driving parameter of our discussion has only to do with taxpayer support; then The Chronicle of Higher Education provides a snapshot looking solely at the 476 public institutions in the U.S.

The Chronicle of Higher Education's website allows information to be sorted by state, type of professor, and numerous other permutations. From any viewpoint, looking at the data or any data by state, the question to be asked is; "are professors being underpaid as originally postulated for the relative value to society?" The parameters of this question offer the following points of observation:

- There is an **oversupply** of available PhD/Doctorate talent.
- Most professors, who study in the pure disciplines, by definition, are very narrow in their knowledge and understanding of the application of that knowledge to the real world.
- As specific disciplines become less STEM (science, technology, engineering and mathematics) oriented, the supply of available talent to teach these subjects enlarges significantly.
- Professors with guaranteed lifetime employment (tenure) can work as long as they wish without fear of dismissal.

The question again arises; per *The Chronicle of Higher Education's Almanac 2014-2015*, **is a 9-month national average salary for tenured professors of $138,500 supportive of a credible argument that faculty trade lifetime employment for lower salaries?** One cannot, in good faith, see the basis for continuing the argument based on salaries alone.

Colleges suffering from economic woes will find it difficult to make management corrections because of guaranteed lifetime employment.

The changes required to transform the underlying economic models of higher education are weighted by the powers of those who are tenured – who are the least concerned with the institution's bottom line – as their job security is guaranteed for life.

Addressing first the supply-demand aspect of those competent enough to teach, it has been shown there is an oversupply of non-tenured PhD/doctorate holding individuals. In a normal economic scenario, this would depress wages. As can be seen, this is not the case. As well, contributing to inflated wages is the time-in-position annual increases and the guaranteed lifetime employment that comes with tenure. Tenure, or guaranteed lifetime employment, from these many perspectives, clearly violates the basic tenants of supply-side economics and again does not appear to have a financial right to exist, nor would it, unless artificially buoyed by tenure practices. It is the public taxpayers and student tuition that allows these practices to continue, as increases in tuition revenue have been the major source of additional funding for both public and private institutions (Dickeson 2).

The truth is, tenured faculty members do not want to have to compete under real-world conditions. There are a number of reasons for this:

- lack of breadth of knowledge,
- inability to add value beyond their specific discipline knowledge,
- the speed of business and industry versus the academy,
- the stress of accountability, and many more.

Tenure avoids this dilemma. By having removed the mandatory retirement age (1994 Federal law), tenure becomes a sole source contract for guaranteed lifetime employment (Hoffer, Sederstrom & Harper 2). Since the 1994 end of mandatory retirement, the average age of retirement has shifted noticeably to the right; with an ever increasing number retiring well past the age of seventy.

Sitting in a meeting on one occasion, a faculty member made mention of working with industry and modifying a curriculum to be more real-world oriented. On hearing this, another more senior faculty member voiced in anger how much he objected to the two world concept, that being academia and the world of business/industry. His rant carried on for ten minutes, seemingly unending. He clearly did not like the idea of being considered less than his business and industry counterparts might perceive him to be.

The short of this example is to recognize that it would never be allowed to happen in business and industry; certainly not more than once. Some senior manager would have sat him down and had a talk with him suggesting he curb his emotional outburst going forward. But, in academia these types of unprofessional and emotionally charged outbursts are allowed under the umbrella of "…that's just how he is…" Keep in mind, this tenured individual cannot be fired, therefore promoting a sense of security allowing these many undesirable behaviors.

On the other hand, what's most interesting is how, when confronted with practices of business and industry, there is a resounding outcry of "...This is academia; it is not a business..." It seems it shouldn't be both ways. The tenured faculty cannot be equal to business and industry only when it is convenient. Ironically, tenured academies **are** truly businesses, albeit not very efficiently run ones; nonetheless they are businesses. More specifically, "...although higher education is a wonderful thing, it is, as a former college president friend of ours reminded us, just another service industry" (Amacher xiii).

It appears from the above data, the argument that faculty are willing to accept lower wages for guaranteed lifetime employment may have had been valid at one time, but is no longer, Asking out loud, how many of our world's educated populace would take an above salary of roughly $100,000 with annual time-in-position increases and accept guaranteed lifetime employment? Can I get a show of hands?

When State Money Dries Up

If this were business and industry, a decline in gross revenue would mean one of two basic things: (a) find new markets in which to sell products and/or services, therefore increasing gross revenue, or alternatively, (b) create efficiencies which in turn reduce costs (and price) to provide the organization's products or services. Academia does not function in this manner.

In public higher education, if costs go up, the college or university simply requests more funding from the state appropriations. If this funding is not made available, then the students bear the brunt through higher tuition and fees.

In reviewing the "Illinois State University's Annual Grapevine Report for 2013", FY 2008 – FY 2013 state cuts to state-specific public institutions of higher education reflect declines as much as 50.4 percent in state spending per student (inflation adjusted). The only two states with increases in state spending per student were Wyoming at +7.5 percent and North Dakota at 16.5 percent. All other states showed declines in state spending per student.

The depicted percent budget cuts in their data are reported (Oliff, 2) to be the result of many economic factors; four of which are discussed below.

First, the U.S. recession from December 2007 through June 2009 resulted in unprecedented and prolonged high unemployment rates. This, coupled with the housing downturn, led to significantly less state revenue collections.

Second, there are more students now than over the last generational cohort (Generation X). The current generation, Generation Y, makes up the school-age population of 18 to 24 year olds.

Although we have documented as many as eight individual cohort groups (Strauss and Howe 36), in practicality, we have four primary age demographic groups in our workforce today (Smith and Clurman, 9; Zemke et al. 3):

- Veterans (1922–1946; 52 million population)
- Boomers (1946–1964; 76 million population)
    - Began turning 65 in January 1, 2011

- Generation X (1964–1980; 44 million population)
- Generation Y (1980–2000; 69.7 million population)

Worth noting, some authors have changed the years associated with the cohort groups, therefore altering the cohort populations. Although The U.S. Census Bureau provides the basic information on live births and birth rates, aside from the Veteran and Boomer cohorts, it is not wholly agreed to exactly which years should be counted in post-Boomer groups, although very few years fluctuate between definitions. Some of the alternative views are premised not as much on number of live births, as they are on seminal events and the age of individuals at the time of those events—keeping in mind a cohort group is typically defined by age and major life-changing and remembered events. Examples of these varying definitions are depicted in the following alternative cohort perspectives:

- Veterans (Traditionalist; 1922–1946; 52 million people who were born prior to WWII)
- Baby Boomers (1946–1964; 76 million people who were born during or after WWII and raised during a period of extreme optimism, opportunity, and progress)
- Generation X'ers (1965–1976; 44 million people who came of age in the shadow of the Boomers; children of older Boomers)
- Generation Y/NeXters (1977–1990; 69.7 million people who are currently the most high-tech and neo-optimistic; most loved)
- Generation Z (1991–present)

Johnson and Johnson (2010, p. 7):

- Veterans (1922–1946; 52 million population)
- Boomers (1946–1964; 76 million population)
- Generation X (1965–1980; 49 million population)
- Generation Y (1981–1995; 70.4 million population)
- Facebook Generation (1995–present)

Plunkett (2010, p. 200):

- The Elderly (pre-1935; 18 million population)
- Pre-Boomers (1935–1945; 23 million population)
- Baby Boomers (1946–1964; 76 million population)
- Generation X (1965–1980; 66 million population)
- Generation Y (1981–2002; 91 million population)
- Diversity Generation (2003+; 32 million population)

In any case, regardless of the definition used above, most of the Veteran cohort group has already retired or are on the verge of doing so. Looking at the year span of this group, 1964 and earlier, we see that the youngest of this group turned 65 in 2011. Behind this group of 52 million are 76 million Boomers, whose oldest just began to turn 60 in 2006 and 65 in January 2011. Clearly, we want to retain the knowledge of the Veteran cohort group, but their exiting the workforce does not form a trough, given the 76 million Boomer backfills.

The trough exists at the next generation down, Generation X, where we move from a population of 76 million Boomers to a forty-two percent reduction of 44 million Generation X'ers, and the gap of scientists and engineers are even greater than the 42 percent decline in the general population. All speculation concerning the shortage of skilled labor in the United States is premised on these numbers and the attendant reduction in working age population.

The NeXters cohort group, even though large in numbers (69.7 million, or 91 million) (Plunkett 5), is not yet fully available or ready to fill the requirements of the gap left by the reduction of Boomers. Beyond NeXters, in comparison to the previous decade, males are marrying later in life from their previous age of 22 to today's age 27, while females are experiencing a comparable move to the right from age 20 to 25 years of age. The average age for first-time mothers in 2001 was 30, whereas the average age for first-time fathers was 32. Some male NeXters even nominate 40 as a good age to become a father (Huntley 182), suggesting another reduction in population may manifest itself in our next documented generation.

Given then, there are more students at this time representing Generation Y than in the last generational cohort, Generation X; thus there are fewer dollars per student to go around. This reduces the average per-student state financial support.

Third, to offset state budget shortfalls and deficits, states have chosen to reduce costs versus increase taxes. Clearly this approach is more palatable to taxpayers. The end result however, is the above-depicted reduction of appropriations to public institutions of higher education. Between 2008 and

TRUTH #1: PROTECTING WHAT DOES NOT HAVE AN ECONOMIC...

2012, states closed 45 percent of the budget gaps through spending cuts, and only 16 percent of their budget gaps through taxes and fees (Oliff 6).

Fourth and last, states used emergency funds, composed of education aid and Medicare funds, to offset their budget deficits through 2011. After 2011, the federal government allowed this type of aid to expire, leaving states reeling for additional sources of efficiencies and funds.

To offset these many budget cuts from the state, public institutions of higher education have resorted to raising student tuition and fees during this same period of FY08 – FY13.

According to the College Board, the percent change in average tuition at public, four-year colleges, inflation adjusted was as high as 78.4 percent. This, with every state reflecting an increase up to this maximum amount.

Notice the difference between the loss of state funding and the rise in student tuition. Just looking at Arizona alone, they lost 50 percent of their state funding and yet raised their tuition by 78 percent. While this is not the case for all state supported public institutions of higher education, it is somewhat clear the loss of state funding directly resulted in increases in student tuition and fees.

Olif states "The decline in state funding and the resulting rise in tuition since the start of the recession have accelerated a longer-term cost shift from states to students and families" (12).

Nobody can disagree with the above statements. There does in fact appear to be a correlation between state funding loss and increases in student tuition and fees. The question, however, is did this have to be the case? It could easily be argued if colleges and universities were run more like businesses, efficiencies could have been found, costs reduced and tuition increases averted. If business/industry received less gross revenue, as previously described, this is exactly what they would have done. Instead of these actions, public supported state universities maintained guaranteed lifetime employment practices, providing guaranteed salaries, and in most cases annual increases for time-in-position (i.e., just for being alive). In other words, if these public universities could easily pass the existing university costs on to students, as evidenced by the above charts, they did exactly that. This is not a model based on accountability – not for business, and certainly not for taxpayer funded public institutions.

Structural Problems with Tenure

Higher education is dominated by government agencies and non-profit organizations. Given this, universities should be expected to be afflicted with major efficiency problems, as return on investment is typically not a requirement. Incentives as well are very different in public and non-profit institutions than in for-profit organizations. There is a significant lack of accountability in public agencies and universities in particular, than in private business and industry. Amacher highlights:

> ...imagine a company that has no profit measure to compare performance year to year or

against competitors. The head of the organization is nominated by a committee process dominated by employees. If the employees become unhappy with the head of the organization, they can demand that he or she be fired – but employees are rarely fired. In essence, that is the world of university governance. The problem is pervasive at state universities (27).

In discussing the structural problems with tenure, the Center for College Affordability and Productivity (CCAP) states:

...tenure enables deadwood and prevents flexibility. The theory of tenure suggests that only those professors who have proven their worth through excellence in teaching, research, and service during the probationary period will be awarded tenure. Such a policy prevents the colleges the flexibility to remove professors who become incompetent or to reallocate labor resources to meet the change in demand for a particular program or discipline. Under most private sector employment policies, when an employee has demonstrated that his/her work no longer meets a minimum standard of quality (and often after efforts to rehabilitate have failed), the employer initiates action to rid itself of the unproductive employee. Under a tenure policy, the employer (college) effectively loses this flexibility to eliminate tenured faculty whose quality of work fails to meet a minimally acceptable level or whose productivity has dwindled over the years. This has often been coined as the deadwood argument" (18).

CCAP talks further about a lack of flexibility brought about by tenure saying:

> **The deadwood problem was exacerbated in 1994 when a federal ban on mandatory faculty retirement went into effect. ... The combination of tenure and the absence of a mandatory retirement age created at least the theoretical specter of aged, unproductive faculty clogging faculty slots that might otherwise have been filled by energetic and freshly trained young scholars...**

> The dynamic nature of the global economy requires that organizations have the flexibility to adapt to changes in the world. The presence of tenure in higher education significantly reduces a college's ability to efficiently reallocate resources in response to consumer demand – a hindrance that would be life-threatening to an organization in a healthy competitive market...

> For instance, courses in information technology or business may be very popular among students, while courses in medieval history

may not. With a tenure system, colleges are not able to reduce the number of medieval history professors in order to increase the number of information technology and business professors, resulting in a misallocation of resources (19).

Universities do not have the type or level of financial measures that organizations in business/industry depend on to drive performance or return investment to shareholders. This in turn allows tenured faculty to act in ways business/industry employees would like to act, but are not allowed to because the market demands accountability and performance, and absolutely does not support sloppy or unproductive practices. ... for colleges, the mission is not to maximize profit, but rather, perhaps, to maximize the quality of their educational output over time. Colleges have no financial market that allows outsiders to evaluate performance or allows a takeover to be mounted to replace a poor quality college board with one that demands better results from top management. There are no shareholders to sue board members who are negligent in the performance of their duties. Poor management of resources at public universities usually produces calls for more taxpayer money to solve the "underfunding" problem (Amacher 29).

In nearly every scenario, university presidents are not expected to be creative or entrepreneurial, especially in comparison to their private company counterparts. A business/industry company president has financial targets and incentives to work toward. University/college presidents, on the other hand, need only do no worse than other peers or aspirational university president colleagues. State colleges/universities simply point to state governments for not providing the required funding. This is a critical difference between business/industry expectations and those for colleges/universities. Business and industry manage to control cost through efficiencies; colleges/universities have no comparable requirement. They simply request more from state coffers, and if not provided, make general "peanut-butter" cuts; these without consideration for long-term efficiencies.

Amacher states:

> In the private sector, change is a fact of life. Call it total quality management, continuous improvement, or reengineering, companies either change and improve or go out of business. The market is touch; if IBM had not cut back its workforce, dumped nonproductive divisions, and made other hard changes, one of the most successful firms on the world in the 1960's and 1970's would have died in the 1990's. Its board and managers did not enjoy the hardship some employees endured and the difficult changes those remaining had to adapt, but these changes brought the company back to life. If IBM had been run like a university, the company would now be a distant memory.
>
> A better analogy to the universities may be the former steel giants that were strangled by union work rules; the union workers were like

professors who resisted changes in productivity and would not accept the fact that the glory days, when PhDs were in hot demand in many disciplines, are over. Real wages in most academic disciplines have fallen; people with at least equal competence would do the same jobs for less. Colleges that can adapt will be more successful than those who are not able to change the incentives facing the biggest cost item – faculty (53).

Perhaps the best way to discuss the financial implications of guaranteed lifetime employment begins with the following

> ...the basic idea is simple: in labor intensive industries such as the performing arts and education, there is less opportunity than other sectors to increase by, for example, substituting capital for labor. Yet markets dictate that, over time, wages for comparably qualified individuals have to increase at roughly the same rate in all industries. As a result, unit labor costs must be expected to rise faster in the performing arts and education than in the economy overall.
>
> While productivity gains have made it possible to assemble cars with only a tiny fraction of the labor that was once required, it still takes four musicians nine minutes to perform Beethoven's No. 4 in C minor, just as it did in the 19th century.

> In short, productivity gains are unlikely to offset wage increases to anything like the same extent in the arts or education as in manufacturing; hence, differential rates of increase in costs are to be expected…(Bowen 5).

This statement was offered as a justification for public higher education continually increasing tuition rates. While understood, how does business and industry handle labor intensive market sectors? They too have this same problem. Yet, they seem to thrive in a very difficult global economy. The answer lies at the root of guaranteed lifetime employment; namely, business/industry does not offer it. People get released from their jobs, they retire, the labor effort is outsourced to other less costly alternative sources of labor, and many other extremely creative solutions.

In academia, however, none of this can happen. **Guaranteed lifetime employment prohibits the turnover of labor. There are no lay-offs, no forced retirements, and few if any restructurings that impact faculty (zero percent unemployment rate once tenured).** There is, however, one disruptive innovation that appears to be infringing on this relic of an employment model; that being massive open online courses (MOOCs). MOOCs, as a disruptive innovation to higher education, will be discussed later in this book.

In one college of a major tier 1 research university, there exists a prime example of how the taxpayer and student tuition is negatively impacted at the hand of guaranteed lifetime employment. In this particular college, there are at least six individuals who teach only one course per semester. Among these six individuals are a previous dean, two replaced associate deans, and three replaced department heads. The cumulative salaries of these individuals, including fringe, is roughly $2.1 million. None of these individuals are any longer in their previous leadership roles, and in fact have been removed and subsequently replaced. Because they are tenured faculty and therefore have guaranteed lifetime employment, they are simply sent back to their home departments to teach as a regular faculty member. Their $2.1 million cumulative salaries represent their faculty salaries after downward adjustments were made from their previously higher administrative salaries. Each of these individuals will be paid this salary, plus annual increases, for the remainder of their desired working lives; some 25 or more years.

If we were to hire an adjunct faculty member who does not have guaranteed lifetime employment, that individual would teach five courses. So it would take 1.2 adjunct faculty members to teach the entire teaching load of the above-mentioned six replaced college leaders. The cost of that 1.2 adjunct full-time equivalent person, including fringe, would be approximately $95,760. If we subtract this figure of $96K from the above $2.1M we have a savings remainder of $2.0M. This means we could, in theory, replace all six of our previously removed and replaced leaders and save $2.0M of taxpayer funding! Unfortunately however, with the existence of guaranteed lifetime employment, we can't. The taxpayer must pay this extra $2.0M and if they refuse, as determined by the state general fund allocations, then the students must pay it. In any case, it must be paid because guaranteed lifetime employment requires it be paid.

In this above scenario, business/industry would handle this situation entirely differently. To begin with, business/industry does not have the luxury of this level of inefficiency or cost-waste. In business/industry there is no "free money" from the state, only the opportunity to raise the cost of products or services; but then, competition contains this option. Most interestingly, the above $2.0M of cost incurred comes at a time when state funding is dwindling and university presidents are professing at lung capacity how state universities have cut expenditures to the bone and can no longer cut expenses without severely impacting curriculum, courses, learning outcomes, and ultimately the overall quality of higher education. This is the moral and ethical evil of guaranteed lifetime employment.

There are numbers upon numbers of arguments against guaranteed lifetime employment (tenure). The most prevalent and recurring arguments say it is an inefficient employment practice that does not have an economic right to exist…period!

Public Perceptions of Tenure

On the public's perception of tenure, Riley writes:

> …tenure hasn't been popular with the public for a while. A 2007 Zogby poll found that 65 percent of respondents agreed with this statement:

"A Professor Who Does Not Have Tenure is More Motivated to Do a Good Job Than One who Does Have Tenure." A 2006 poll by the American Association of University Professors found that more than two-thirds of the public thinks tenure should be modified, and 13 percent think it should be eliminated (6).

On Wednesday, February 23, 2011, the Rep. Christopher Herrod of Utah put forth a bill that would end tenure in the state of Utah. The bill, HB485, was defeated by a margin of 9-3, but not without making a growing point of the sentiment of the people of that state.

> SALT LAKE CITY — A bill that would prevent state universities from offering tenure to future professors failed to advance on a 9-3 vote Wednesday in the House Education Committee. HB485 sponsoring Rep. Christopher Herrod, R-Provo, said he believes a free market, competitive approach results in the best people competing for jobs, and tenure runs contrary to that principal. "No one is entitled to guaranteed employment," Herrod said.
>
> The Utah County Republican told the committee tenure is expensive and professorships shouldn't be promised, especially in times of economic hardship. "There's nothing we can do with those

individuals who currently have tenure," he said. "We have this large, unfunded liability."

University officials spoke in opposition to the legislation, including William Sederburg, Utah's commissioner of higher education. "Passage of this bill will really be damaging to the state of Utah," Sederburg told the committee. Herrod's concern that poor professors are being guaranteed a job isn't as big of a problem as alleged, Sederburg said. If anything, tenure helps secure the best of the best, he said. "Many, many, many faculty members are weeded out in that process," he said. "It is very much a minority of professors that have tenure." Sederburg also told the committee schools can revoke tenure in times of financial strain, or as a result of poor performance.

Herrod amended the bill since it was first introduced. He made an allowance for the state's two research universities, the University of Utah and Utah State University, to enter into 10-year contracts with professors. Rep. Kay McIff, R-Richfield, voted against the bill, saying it would weaken Utah's appeal to the best and brightest professors. "Right now, the world is organized in such a way that I think we would put our institutions at a disadvantage," he said (2).

Bowen makes the case for public sentiment by saying

> ...it seems to me, as to many others, that people in general are fed up with rising costs, and especially rising student charges, however understandable the reason for them may be... the anger and resentment expressed towards college leaders appear to be growing, despite the limited ability of those leaders to make college cheaper quickly... no part of higher education is immune from the consequences of ignoring this rising tide of anger and resentment (26)... there is a definite political aspect to all this. We must recognize if higher education does not begin to slow the rate of increase in college costs, our nation's higher education system will lose the public support on which it so heavily depends. There has been an undeniable erosion of public trust in the capacity of higher education to operate more efficiently (63).

As reported by The Chronicle of Higher education, January 13, 2017, two additional bills were introduced in the states of Iowa and Missouri.

"...Senator Brad Zaun of Iowa and state Rep. Rick Brattin of Missouri — proposed bills this month that would eliminate the tenure system at public colleges and universities. Missouri House Bill 266 isn't exclusively about cutting tenure. The bill would also require public colleges to publish estimated costs of degrees, employment opportunities expected for graduates, average salaries of previous graduates, and a summary of the job market, among other things. In an interview with The Chronicle, Mr. Brattin said that tenure is "outdated" and hinders colleges from holding professors accountable. Professors' main focus should be to help students get the best job possible, he said. "Something's wrong, something's broken, and a professor that should be educating our kids should be concentrating on ensuring that they're propelling to a better future, but instead are engaging in political stuff that they shouldn't be engaged in," Mr. Brattin said.

In Iowa, Mr. Zaun's bill focuses specifically on getting rid of tenure in public universities and community colleges, giving the Iowa Board of Regents more power, and establishing a program to hire more female faculty in "targeted shortage areas." Iowa Senate Bill 41 proposes to eliminate tenure completely, including for current faculty. The Missouri bill would stop awarding tenure after January 1, 2018, but does not say it will eliminate tenure for current employees."

Providing guaranteed lifetime employment, in the eyes of the public, at a time when unemployment is hovering around eight percent and people change jobs anywhere from eight to twelve times in their careers, just doesn't seem fair. When everyone else is struggling to make ends meet, living through recessions as best they can, guaranteeing someone lifetime employment, again, just doesn't seem fair. To repeat, no country or business provides this level of security. Tenure, guaranteed lifetime employment, simply runs against those who produce more and have to compete more in a continually evolving global economy. The public is beginning to move from apathy to resentment of what appears an under-serving and economically infeasible and indefensible benefit.

Managing Human Resources – Tenure, Unions, Everybody Else

Managing employees (human resources) is different when talking about those who are tenured versus those in a union and all the rest who are neither tenured or in an organized union.

Some of the many characteristics that identify nonprofit organizations are strongly related to tax implications. Other of those characteristics have to do with how profit is handled, the mission of the organization, the oversight of the board of directors, and the source of funding.

Nonprofit organizations charge for products, services, or memberships. Some of these nonprofits generate significant amounts of profit; this is allowable and ideal as is the scenario for any business. The difference is the profits are not passed on to shareholders; instead, the profits are reinvested back into the nonprofit organization to advance the mission. This is how nonprofits are allowed to grow. All of their costs are covered as expenses and the remaining profits (commonly called residuals in nonprofit organizations) are simply reapplied as deemed acceptable for continued growth of the organization.

The mission of nonprofits is typically different from for-profit organizations in business/industry. In nonprofits, their mission is typically to serve the greater public or social good. This is exhibited in organizations that work in health care (hospitals), education (k12, colleges and universities), churches, community programs, or foundations with one or more purposes (Nahavandi 249).

Business and industrial organizations have a board of directors that is made up of paid individuals. These many individuals are typically highly experienced and bring some form of discipline-specific knowledge to the organization through their involvement. Nonprofit organizations, on the other hand, have a board of directors who are not paid. Although they may bring significant discipline-specific knowledge to the table, they may also simply have a burning passion to be part of the organization, which, in the end, creates strong advocates for the nonprofit's mission.

Like businesses, nonprofits may charge a fee for their products or services. Generally, however, nonprofits' primary funding sources are through contributions, grants, donations, agency and industry funding and foundations.

There are hundreds of organizations worldwide that meet the definition of being nonprofits. A few of the top 100 include National Public Radio (NPR), United Nation's Children Fund (UNICEF), Smithsonian Institute, World Food Program – USA, American Cancer Society, Save the Children, Feed America, and many more.

On leadership challenges of nonprofit organizations, Nahavandi notes:

The leadership of nonprofit organizations involves the same principles as other organizations. Their leaders must help individuals and groups set goals and guide them in the achievement of those goals. The public-good mission of nonprofits, along with the voluntary participation of many of their employees, contributors, and other stakeholders, create a particular burden on leaders of such organizations to lead through a collaborative and trust-based style. In most cases, individual donors, except for their tax benefits when applicable, do not get tangible benefits from their donation and the resources they contribute do not always stay in their community...

As much as integrity, trustworthiness, and self-sacrifice are elements for all leadership situations, they are even more so in the nonprofit organizations. Without the profit motive, which legitimately guides business organizations, and the rewarding of its leaders (e.g., top leaders being compensated with company shares), the nonprofit organizations are likely to attract leaders with a stronger focus on civic contribution...

One of the major challenges that leaders of nonprofit organizations face is how to recruit, retain, and motivate employees, many of whom are volunteers, without having access to substantial monetary rewards. Even in the case of paid employees, salaries are often lower than comparable positions in business organizations. The leaders of nonprofits, therefore, require considerable skills in motivating and inspiring their followers. In many cases, followers have joined the nonprofit because they are passionate about its mission; however, passion alone does not always lead to effectiveness. An additional factor is that the structure of many nonprofits is relatively flat with few employees and few layers of management. Effective leadership requires empowerment, effective use of all resources available, often by harnessing the power of teams, and participation to creatively solve problems without many resources (252).

There are numerous subtleties from the above observations. First, relative to individuals who participate in nonprofit organizations, they are not typically paid, or in the least, not paid very highly. This lends itself to the argument in academia that tenured faculty are not paid as those in business/industry and therefore should be entitled to guaranteed lifetime employment. This issue is discussed when we discuss salaries of tenured faculty at all levels versus others who are not tenured. *The premise tenured faculty are paid less is simply not true.*

Second, those individuals who wish to participate in nonprofits, which assumes colleges and universities as well, wish to do so because they are serving the greater good. While this may be true, it does not imply guaranteed lifetime employment is required in order for them to do so. There are many examples throughout this text which demonstrate highly competent and talented individuals participate in public institutions of higher education without having guaranteed lifetime employment.

Third and perhaps most notably, whether in business or non-profits, there is the opportunity for leadership to react to a burning platform. This means moving resources where needed, increasing support in areas of weaknesses, eliminating those activities or initiatives that are a monetary drag on the interests of the whole organization and other efficiency-gaining opportunities in an effort to serve their stated missions. This is not the case in public institutions of higher education which have a tenure system and tenured faculty. Tenure, as discussed above, runs counter to the burning platform effect. It creates a sense of entitlement which contributes to the many previously documented evils: unprofessional behavior, immaturity and passive, if not openly, aggressive behavior. Leadership in public institutions of higher education cannot make the required changes for efficiency when shackled by the vote of those not inclined to participate- those who feel compelled to maintain the status quo. This is why leadership in those organizations with a tenure system appears to be hand-tied to mediocrity and basic management versus true leadership and change facilitation.

CHAPTER 2

Truth #2: Implications of Entitlement; No Burning Platform, No Sense of Urgency

"The credit belongs to the man who is actually in the arena, whose face is marred by dust and sweat and blood; who strives valiantly; who errs, and comes short again and again, because there is no effort without error and shortcoming; but who...spends himself in a worthy cause; who, at the best knows in the end the triumph of high achievement, and who at the worst, if he fails, at least fails while daring greatly, so that his place will never be with those cold and timid souls who know neither victory nor defeat." Theodore Roosevelt

While attending Mass one Saturday evening, Fr. Patrick made the statement "...[if we all knew we were going to get into heaven regardless, then what incentive would we necessarily have to live by God's commandments, be kind to others, or avoid any other ills]..."

Throughout business/industry the impetus for immediate change is frequently called a "burning platform". The figure below is but one figure depicting this concept. In fact, the phrase is so common; an image such as that below can readily be acquired from a search of Google images. The burning platform is a visual image which instills a sense of urgency; a sense of immediacy.

FIGURE 2.1

The burning platform creates a call to action. It shocks us into wanting to do something, recognizing no action would

TRUTH #2: IMPLICATIONS OF ENTITLEMENT; NO BURNING...

certainly be to our detriment and potential demise. The burning platform rallies our collective efforts toward that which will make us once again safe and secure. We recognize in its image, a catastrophic and cataclysmic fate.

Generally, tenured faculty do not readily recognize the burning platform context. For that matter, only superficial attempts to silence the temporary cries for transformation are readily recognized. Higher tuition rates, poor social or economic conditions, increasingly greater debt loads of graduating seniors and the like have little to no emotional impact on tenured faculty. They don't see, or perhaps more appropriately "feel" the immediacy of the situation. And, again, why should they? Remember; they have guaranteed lifetime employment, guaranteed salary, and guaranteed salary increases for time-in-position for the rest of their working lives, which is when they decide to quit working, if at all.

There is danger in the comfort zone. Becoming comfortable creates many ills. When too much is provided to individuals with no expectation of accountability, it is easy to feel a sense of entitlement. In business and industry, entitlement can develop as a result of poor management. This happens when managers want to avoid the confrontations that result from holding people responsible for outcomes.

In any work environment, people feel a sense of entitlement when they do not have to earn or work for their rewards or benefits. The root cause of entitlement stems from many things, most notably:

- when employees collect paychecks on a regular and expected basis whether they produce a lot of output or a little
- when raises are given for nothing more than time-in-position
- when there is a sense of guaranteed lifetime employment
- when no formal process exists for measuring performance or none that has any real impact
- when the emphasis is on traditions
- when a compensation system does not really reflect an individual's contributions
- in light of a formal hierarchy where differences in status dictate overall behavior

When people do not have to earn what they get, when it is already there, they very soon take for granted that which they receive. The tragic human irony is that they are not grateful for what they get. Instead, they want something more; this is the premise of entitlement.

In her book, *Danger in the Comfort Zone*, Bardwick states:

> [Too much security] "...I've worked here a long time and have done what you expected. I've earned my security." That is the working presumption of a majority of people who work in our various government bodies, in all levels of our schools, in our large and powerful unions, and in our mature and prosperous corporations. It amounts to total

job security. Too much security is what entitlement is all about.

Some groups of people have formal tenure. They set a precedent for others to argue their right to have the same certainty. In recent years those precedents became transformed into court decisions so it can become legally difficult to fire people (28).

Increasingly, when job security is absolute, there is no reason to have performance reviews. To this end, organizations that provide this level of guaranteed lifetime employment stray further and further from these performance related measurements. Quite simply, because they are instruments to measure performance, they are not required when guaranteed lifetime employment exists. "This is the truly insidious danger of entitlement: it settles in everywhere and becomes part of the mortar that holds everything together (Bardwick x)."

A story applicable to this discussion follows:

While yet in high school and in his first year attending college, Noah worked part-time in a grocery store. Noah had grown up in a very poor and bad environment and his family was routinely without the necessities of life. They were by all standards very, very poor. Noah was blessed with a strong work ethic, most likely stemming from his not wanting to ever be poor. He realized at an early age that hard work provided opportunity, which in turn provided the much-cherished financial resources that eluded him and his family at an early age.

Noah worked upwards of 30 hours per week while in high school; every night and most all weekends. If he had a school holiday or break, such as summer or Christmas, Noah would ask for more hours and felt grateful for his monetary rewards. At work in the grocery store, Noah was perceived as a high achiever. While most others managed just one aisle, Noah had three. At one point Noah managed three aisles and was the dairy manager, all at the same time. Noah, by any definition, was a worker.

The grocery store was unionized. Noah was forced to be part of the union and pay his union dues as were all others. Noah didn't like paying these dues and one day went to his local union hall and asked that he be allowed to withdraw from the union. To this request, the union representative said they would look into it and sent Noah away thinking he had perhaps extricated himself from these monthly withdrawals.

The next day, Noah was called into the store manager's office. Noah got along very well with the store manager and did not see this as anything necessarily unusual. This time, however, was different. The store manager told Noah that he had been contacted by the local union hall about Noah's visit. Noah acknowledged the visit. The store manager asked that Noah not do this, as it made waves for the store, the store manager, and perhaps others. Noah didn't say anything and left the store manager's office.

TRUTH #2: IMPLICATIONS OF ENTITLEMENT; NO BURNING...

Noah wasn't convinced he was in the wrong and still did not like the perceived excessive union dues being removed. To this end, Noah went back to the union hall that afternoon. He told the union hall representative about the store manager's conversation and reiterated he did not want to be part of the union. Noah asked the union representative to quit removing union dues from his check for a second time. To this, the union representative invited Noah to a weekend cookout where they would have hamburgers and drinks. Noah was a minor, did not like alcohol, and graciously thanked the representative for the invitation, but declined; besides, Noah had to work on both weekend days as he had done for so long.

The next business day, the store manager once again called Noah into his office. This time the store manager was firmer and told Noah he must stop asking to be removed from the union that it would have some very negative ramifications on a lot of people, perhaps including Noah himself.

Noah was a tad put off by this firmer lecture from his store manager. He did not know what to do. In the store was a nightly security guard who was actually a police officer with the city. Noah liked the police officer and struck up a conversation on the topic. The police officer told Noah the state was a right-to-work state and Noah did not have to be part of the union by law. Noah didn't know if this was true or not and really did not understand the right-to-work state topic anyway, but Noah did hear what he wanted to hear which was that he did not have to be part of the union if he did not wish to be.

Armed with this new information, Noah went back to the union hall a third time and once again confronted the union hall representative on the matter. Noah explained he had talked with a police officer friend of his and had learned that he did not have to be part of the union if he did not wish to be… and that was the law. Noah left after that discussion thinking this was truly the end of this and he would get his union dues restored to his paycheck on a weekly basis.

Noah was very confident in his abilities. He knew he worked harder and did more than the others and felt he could find another job if something bad were to happen. To this end, Noah did not feel concerned over his financial well-being in this particular job.

Two days had gone by and Noah had not heard anything from his store manager, so Noah naturally thought this was complete and all was well. Then, in walked the individual from headquarters that seldom came around unless something was wrong. Noah watched him as he came straight into the store and into the store manager's office. Noah was concerned over seeing this; he suspected, given his third trip to the union hall, that this could be about him.

Minutes had passed, which seemed like forever, and Noah heard his named called over the intercom to come to the stock room. The stock room was where the entire inventory was kept. It was very large, all concrete, and not a very welcoming area. All the same, Noah went. On arrival, he saw the store department head and the headquarters' manager.

TRUTH #2: IMPLICATIONS OF ENTITLEMENT; NO BURNING...

Noah wasn't sure exactly what to expect, but he knew this had the potential to be his last day on the job. Nervously, Noah approached the two men and stood quietly. Noah was asked to sit down on a jury-rigged chair from boxes of canned goods. The very tall headquarters' manager began by saying that he understood Noah had been visiting the union hall and asking that he not be forced to pay union dues. To this Noah replied that was true. The headquarters' manager asked why Noah felt compelled to do this three times, even after he had been asked by his store manager not to do so. Noah explained that he ran three aisles and was the dairy manager and felt he did not need the protection the union hall provided to the others who produced much less than he. Noah said he did not hold it against others for their wanting to be part of the union, but that he did not feel he needed the protection they provided.

Noah expected the worse. The next thing out of the manager's mouth from headquarters floored Noah. The headquarters' manager said "...son, you are a tremendous asset. We like you and your work ethic. We would like to make you an assistant manager..." On hearing this, Noah about fell off his boxes. Did he hear this right? Was he being offered an assistant manager job? The headquarters' manager went on to say "...you will be given another 25 cents per hour and most importantly you will no longer have to be in the union, so you will be getting the union dues paid back into your weekly paycheck." Noah was ecstatic! He was now an assistant store manager, he received a raise, no longer had to pay union dues and everyone appeared happy. What a deal!

In talking to Noah, he was clearly driven by an underlying fear; the fear of being poor: his burning platform. Noah had been poor his whole life. He could tell stories that would make grown men and women tear up. Noah learned from an early age that hard work would make him more valuable, which in turn created opportunities and overall would lessen the chance he would ever be poor again. In his case, Noah turned his underlying fear into action. Noah's call to action, or burning platform, was the constant fear of being poor. Noah did not assume he was entitled, he instead, recognized hard work would produce desired results; higher pay, and, more secured employment.

In discussing what entitlement costs us, Bardwick explains:

> The dollar cost of entitlement packages to entitled employees is only one reason we cannot afford to tolerate the conditions of entitlement. The real cost to our nation is the loss of creativity, innovation, and creative thinking… people are not at their keenest when life is too safe. When people receive without having to achieve, they are protected from failure. There is no punishment for not achieving…. By protecting people from risk, we destroy their self-esteem. We rob them of the opportunity to become strong competent people. Facing risk is the only way we gain confidence, because confidence is the result of mastering challenge. Confidence is an internal state. It cannot be given, it can only be earned… thus too

little anxiety is destructive. It deprives people of the experiences that create confidence.

Instead of strength, courage, and confidence, people trapped by entitlement are cautious and avoid risk. When security is very high and people shouldn't be afraid, they are. Entitled people cling to entitlement, fearing they couldn't earn or compete or survive on their own. The long-term result of too much protection is an endless search for protection because we are afraid of losing it (27).

When people are **not** held accountable for performance, they do **not** perform. Instead, they can become complacent; this given no performance criteria is required of them. Productivity is always lowest among those who feel a sense of entitlement.

We must shake loose the psychology of entitlement. We must empower people by giving them responsibilities, and we must hold them accountable for their actions. Only in this way can we engender the achievement, growth, and confidence that are necessary for maximum productivity (29).

Unfortunately, whenever entitlement exists in an organization, it is usually because it has been established as part of the culture. This is why it usually takes a significant shock or call to action to gain the appropriate motivation to act. Given that moving away from entitlement creates a risk, there will always be an element of fear to overcome.

Bardwick goes on to describe the relationship between entitlement, earning, and fear. Bardwick depicts productivity as being very low when anxiety is either very low or very high. *Relative to earnings, when security is dependent on producing, or output, productivity is at its highest.* On entitlement, Bardwick suggests avoiding risk and creating safety are institutionalized in rules and procedures. In this scenario, appearance is more important than achievement. When fear is present, there is no sense of having any control; resulting in people panicking and creating a sense of every person for themselves.

Generally, *people resist leaving the comfort of entitlement.* When they are pushed out of it, they will try to return. The only real way to energize apathetic organizations is to push them into the psychology of earning. After years of avoiding risk, most people will find this distasteful. Only a call to action, or burning platform effect, will move people and organizations out of entitlement.

To summarize, with guaranteed lifetime employment, guaranteed salary, annual increases for time-in-position, and a zero (0) percent unemployment rate, where is the burning platform for change?

There has been a lot of work done that discusses the relationship between competition, self-control, and innovation. Bronson and Merryman, in their book *Top Dog,* address this very natural phenomenon. They analyzed the saliva samples of those who skydive and those who ballroom dance. In looking first at the skydivers, they discovered skydivers had a huge rush of stress on the first jump, but succeeding lower levels of rush stress on the second and third jumps. The authors concluded "...the true 'high' of skydiving, and other edgeworks, stems from the way skilled performance brings control to a situation most people would regard as uncontrollable" (5). This sense of control stems from the skydiver's capacity to focus attention on the actions necessary for survival. "The feeling of self-determination they get from conquering the risks is the real payoff. It is not pure thrill they seek, but the ability to control the environment within a thrilling context (5)."

When the authors looked at ballroom dancers, they found something unexpected. The ballroom dancers did not experience the fall-off of rush stress the skydivers had. No matter how many times they competed, the rush stress was always high.

> ...according to what science tells us, dancing at that point in their lives should have required very little cognitive control. All of the muscle memory should have been driven down into the cerebellum region of their brains, where it was automated. There should have been no worry over forgetting to vary the inside and outside of their feet to create style and line... but that wasn't the case. The intense stress reaction was no different between the [groups tested]. The cutthroat world of ballroom dancing remained

terrifying no matter how long they'd been at it. The contestants did not habituate. But how is it that someone can get used to skydiving but not ballroom dancing? Because the real difference between skydiving and ballroom dancing isn't defined by the physical environment of the activities. It is not even about the actual jeopardy to life and limb. The real difference between skydiving and ballroom dancing was the psychological environment. The expert dancers were in competition and the skydivers were not. To be more precise, it isn't the dancing that is stress inducing, it is being judged. It was winning and losing (8).

This argument suggests the rivalry creates a sense of competitiveness. Competitiveness is what causes people to come out swinging; to do the hard things; to put their noses to the grindstone and produce when required. Competitiveness turns *external* energy into *internal* energy; it is the visualization of purpose, the thing which makes us all want to be part of the solution and put forth maximum effort. Even if there is no burning platform, competitiveness and the internalization of the stated purpose provide unparalleled impetus to do more, and to get ahead of our competitors. Competition spurs motivation (18).

It is also true that competition increases the creative side of motivation. Competition "...doesn't kill creativity; it facilitates creative output by supplying motivational drive. Competition teaches people to be comfortable with conflict and opposition; these are necessary building blocks for developing the creative psyche" (19).

Success in competition requires taking risks, which are normally held back by fear. Those protected by guaranteed lifetime employment have never had to learn how to compete with integrity and honor. This is why so many non-tenured faculty will testify to the tremendous immaturity and lack of professionalism within the tenured ranks. Most who witness this readily recognize it would never be tolerated in business/industry. To these many incidents we simply respond, "...well that's so and so; you know how he/she is..." What is really being said is that we can't do anything about it; they have guaranteed lifetime employment and it's not worth the corrective action pursuit!

The authors of *Top Dog* take the relationship between competition, self-control, and innovation to the next level by postulating how competition leads to self-improvement, which in turn leads directly to greater innovation and performance. They state "...the real benefit of competition is not winning – it is improved performance... competitors discover an extra gear... competition facilitates improvement" (27).

The Matthew Effect and the Mark Effect have been coined to address an interesting dichotomy of assisting those who are competitively oriented from those who do not do as well under such stress.

> ...The term Matthew Effect was coined by sociologist Robert Merton in 1968; it refers to the

dynamic that the early leaders in a competition tend to get showered with resources that make them even better, increasing the gap on weaker competitors over time. For instance, the best students get sent to the best schools, where they have the best teachers; in the same way the best players get sent to the best teams, where they get trained by the best coaches. The term was inspired by the Gospel According to Matthew: "For to everyone who has, more will be given and he will grow rich; but from the one who has not, even what he has will be taken away" (40).

Whenever we try to counteract this, whenever we try to distribute resources to prop up the weaker competitors – we're applying the Mark Effect. The term was coined in 2009 by the University of Chicago's Matthew Bothner, drawing from the Gospel According to Mark: "But the first will be last, and the last will be first." In our society, there's almost an unlimited number of ways we try to assist, or intervene, when competitors are unequal. We take it as a given that competition is predicated on a level playing field – that the rules apply to all, and if some redistribution isn't done now and then, the rich will just get richer to the point there is no competition left [too big a gap between those with and those without, thus eliminating the psychological effect of competition] (40).

In some theoretical and practical sense, *guaranteed lifetime employment has weakened the competitive spirit of those with it to the point they do not feel they can compete in the "real-world".* **Therefore,** *they both depend upon and defend their perceived right to the security afforded by guaranteed lifetime employment.*

Recently, Daniel Paquette changed the perceptions of social psychology by proposing against the micro-monitoring of "helicopter parents". He argued that attachment theory has overvalued a parent's role in providing comfort when children feel insecure. Equally, it has undervalued the parent's role in fostering exploratory behavior. He noted that studies of animals deprived of rough and tumble play show they grow up unable to be successfully aggressive: they perceive threats when there are none, and they do not perceive any when they should (119). Paquette explains that parents who allow modulated and controlled aggression teach their children how to reasonably express that aggression.

This is not the scenario with those who possess guaranteed lifetime employment. Modulation and control is seldom exercised. Instead, the behavior is ignored. Instead of instruction and counsel producing acceptable outcomes, ignoring the behavior simply reinforces bad behavior. The important thing about monitored roughhousing, explains Paquette, is that the parent maintains control. The children are allowed to be animated, but the parents help de-escalate potential problems when kids are on the brink of anger or frustration (119).

On April 11, 2014, "ASEE First Bell", an on-line electronic newsletter for members of the American Society for Engineering Education, identified one of their daily top articles as:

Community Colleges Begin Offering Bachelor Degrees Across US

"The Hechinger Report" (Marcus) reports that community colleges in 21 states are now able to issue bachelor's degrees and have started offering degrees in high demand subjects. In Florida, the number of students entering community colleges has grown to 30,000, many attracted by the tuition, which is significantly cheaper than four-year universities. The trend has been opposed by four-year universities, who have lobbied against community college degree expansion in Colorado, Michigan, and California. Florida Sen. Joe Negron (R-28 District) proposed halting the expansion of community college bachelor programs leading Kenneth Walker, founder and former chairman of the Community College Baccalaureate Association, to say the debate "comes down to the money. And from my perspective, the focus ought to be on meeting the needs of the students, meeting the needs of business and industry." The article notes that California will begin allowing its students to receive bachelor degrees at community colleges to address a predicted shortfall in 2025.

TRUTH #2: IMPLICATIONS OF ENTITLEMENT; NO BURNING...

This article led to numerous others of similar content. The topic throughout the many articles described how 21 of the 50 states in the U.S. had provided their respective community colleges the right to offer bachelor's degrees. Community colleges, by their nature, usually stop at an associate degree. Participants in these associate degrees then have the opportunity to transfer to a four-year college or university, should they choose to do so.

A series of articles by Clayton Christensen implies that the new regulations may relegate applied technology degrees to more affordable community colleges. The expensive university level education is then left to focus on research.

Another example of the inefficiency created by "tenure-mentality" was revealed in a recent discussion with a peer university college department head. He was venting over the lack of support he was getting from his faculty. He commented how two years earlier, three of his four academic degree programs were on the list of red programs, meaning they had a negative return on investment due to low enrollments.

For the last two years his organization had attempted to re-model these troubled programs. Their solution was simple and somewhat Machiavellian. The faculty had chosen to create an umbrella degree with these three programs as tracks within. The hope was that enrollment for the newly combined three programs would be sufficient to stave off additional scrutiny from senior leadership. Unfortunately, enrollments were continuing their downward spiral. This lead to the perception that nobody wanted the degree programs now any more than before.

I asked if the faculty felt any sense of urgency, perhaps concern over their employment, due to the threatening enrollment status. To this he said, "No, none at all"; his faculty seemed unintimidated. Subsequent to this, we discussed the potential outside threat from community colleges to his programs, and for that matter to all programs within this college. Again, he said the faculty had no fear or concerns whatsoever. He pointed out that in all prior years, since the college's inception, no faculty member had ever been fired for low enrollments, failed programs, or other academically related reasons; so given this, why should they be concerned now? He commented that, not only were they unconcerned, but saw no reason to do anything more than what they currently did... just for fewer students.

The Politics of Entitlement

Politics are different in business and industry than they are in institutions of higher learning. I was warned before coming to work for academia that the politics would be beyond anything I had ever experienced. Those warnings were so very correct.

There is a very good reason for the politics of academia being so pronounced and unjustifiably ferocious: entitlement stemming from guaranteed lifetime employment. A lack of fear has the potential to birth a lack of professionalism and considerable immaturity, which it does with incomparable emphasis!

In business and industry, there are politics as well; many times I have had my lunch eaten by others more capable of political maneuvering than I. However, there are also checks and balances to shut down too much of this political, Machiavellian behavior.

Generally, when someone feels that their lowest level of Maslow's hierarchy – namely food, clothing, and shelter – is in question, they tend to take notice of this potential and behave in a more congenial manner. Alternately, if they persist in these misguided patterns of behavior, they will be looking for other employment.

In academia, however, it is much different. Faculty and faculty administrators recognize the realities of how hard it is to remove a tenured faculty member. The process is a costly and lengthy one of a yearlong or more. To this end, administrators simply ignore the behavior or write it off as being the misbehaving individual's character; which, in the end, simply reinforces the undesirable behavior, no matter how bad it may be.

Given, then, the lack of accountability, coupled with an underlying psychology of lifetime employment, behaviors that would normally be considered unprofessional, immature, and sometimes-borderline civil actions, are tolerated and, by default, encouraged.

Tenured faculty blatantly, intentionally, and willingly participate in the politics of higher education. Guaranteed lifetime employment promotes the absolute worst behavior of any ever witnessed in business or industry. Knowing there is no threat of being fired, salary security and annual increases for time-in-position promote and propagate unchecked and unreasonable behaviors.

Fear – From Paralysis to Power

FEAR

"I am Fear. I am the menace that lurks in the paths of life, never visible to the eye but sharply felt in the heart. I am the father of despair, the brother of procrastination, the enemy of progress, the tool of tyranny. Born of ignorance and nursed on misguided thought, I have darkened more hopes, stifled more ambitions, shattered more ideals and prevented more accomplishments than history could record.

Like the changing chameleon, I assume many disguises. I masquerade as caution. I am sometimes known as doubt or worry. But whatever I'm called, I am still fear, the obstacle of achievement.

I know no master but one; its name is Understanding. I have no power but what the human mind gives me, and I vanish completely when the light of Understanding reveals the facts as they really are, for I am really nothing."

TRUTH #2: IMPLICATIONS OF ENTITLEMENT; NO BURNING...

> *You see, if you have the courage to acknowledge your fears, you will be taking the first step toward controlling them instead of them controlling you. And if you take the next step toward understanding, you will be able to move past them to empathy, perhaps even to love.*
>
> — Lou Tice

Fear is a natural human emotional state. It causes us to act, or in some cases, to not act at all. It creates a scenario where decisions that should be made, are not. Fear and its implications have been well documented.

Susan Jeffers, in her book *Feel the Fear and Do It Anyway* states:

> ...you may be surprised and encouraged to learn that while inability to deal with fear may look and feel like a psychological problem, in most cases it isn't. I believe it is primarily an educational problem, and that by reeducating the mind, you can accept fear as simply a fact of life rather than a barrier to success (4)...

Fear, according to Jeffers, may be broken into three levels as depicted in the following table.

LEVEL 1 FEARS	
Those that Happen	**Those that Require Action**
aging	going back to school
becoming disabled	making decisions
retirement	changing a career
being alone	making friends
children leaving home	ending or beginning a relationship
natural disasters	using the phone
loss of financial security	asserting oneself
change	losing weight
dying	being interviewed
war	driving

FIGURE 2.2

Unlike Level 1 fears, level 2 fears are not situation-oriented; they involve the ego.

LEVEL 2 FEARS	
rejection	being conned
success	helplessness
failure	disapproval
being vulnerable	loss of image

FIGURE 2.3

Level 3 Fear is the essence of all fear; it is solidly premised on one main theme … "I can't handle what will happen to me… (15)" If you test this hypothesis, look at how Level 1 Fears translate:

- I can't handle illness
- I can't handle making a mistake
- I can't handle losing my job
- I can't handle getting old
- I can't handle being alone
- I can't handle making a fool out of myself
- I can't handle not getting the job
- I can't handle losing him/her
- I can't handle losing my money…

Level 2 Fear translates into:

- I can't handle the responsibility of success
- I can't handle failure
- I can't handle being rejected

From all of this, Level 3 simply says "I can't handle it!" The truth is: if you knew you could handle anything that came your way, what would you possibly have to fear? The answer is nothing!

According to Jeffers, there are five basic truths about fear:

Truth #1 – fear will never go away as long as we continue to grow. As long as we continue to push out into the world, to stretch our capabilities, and as long as we continue to take risks to help make our dreams come true, we will always have some element of fear.

Truth #2 – the only way to get rid of the fear of doing something is to go out and do it. Fear of a given situation dissolves when we confront it. "Doing something" has to precede the diminishing of the fear.

Truth #3 – the only way to feel better about ourselves is to go out and do something. The "doing it" part has to come before we can feel better about ourselves. Once we take action, not only does the fear begin to subside, but we gain a whole new sense of self-confidence.

Truth #4 – not only does each of us experience fear when confronted with a new and unfamiliar situation, but so does everyone else in a similar, unfamiliar situation.

Truth #5 – pushing through fear is less frightening than living with the underlying fear that stems from a feeling of helplessness. This basically says "…no matter how secure any of us feel in our little self-constructed cocoon, we live, consciously or unconsciously, with the fear that the day of reckoning will eventually come" (28).

Jeffers says "…if everybody feels fear when approaching something new in life, yet so many are out there "doing it" despite the fear, then we must conclude that fear is not the problem (33)." The obvious secret is to move from a position of paralysis to a position of power. Doing this is not easy:

> …The outlook, attitudes, self-images, and ways of thinking that were functional in the past have to "die" before people can be ready for life in the present. Moses took care of

TRUTH #2: IMPLICATIONS OF ENTITLEMENT; NO BURNING...

transition's ending phase when he led his people out of Egypt, but it was the forty years in the neutral zone wilderness that got Egypt out of his people. You aren't going to be able to do it in a few weeks either (Bridges 43).

One of the ways I suggest people deal with fear is to visualize the worst-case scenario of the fear at hand. In viewing the worst-case scenario, ask yourself "...how would I deal with this should it materialize?" If you can visualize facing, experiencing, and ultimately resolving the situation, then you will begin to gain a sense of control and power over the fear. Note that in reality the worst-case scenario rarely materializes as visualized and a path of lesser impact is taken. The point being, we must feel a sense of power over the situation to better address it and to overcome the fear associated with it.

Heller (5) describes the differences between normal and abnormal fear responses as follows.

> **...Normal fear:** a state of alarm or dread to prepare you to flee, fight, or freeze. Necessary for survival, it mobilizes you to take action to protect yourself from threats.
>
> **Irrational fear:** a powerful feeling of peril when little or no real danger threatens.
>
> **Anxiety:** a vague feeling of fear and apprehension that creates unease. Although feeling

agitated, you may not be able to put into words what actually threatens you.

Phobia: a disrupting or persistent fear of an object or an idea that is out of proportion to any proposed danger. You know it is ridiculous to fear bees, but feel helpless to control the fear.

Panic: a sudden surge of acute terror, as John Madden feels while flying in an airplane (7).

In defending guaranteed lifetime employment, people take action or inaction based on their perception of what could be. It is not uncommon that our imagination runs wild visualizing all the catastrophic things that can happen. This "catastrophisizing" creates anticipatory anxiety, paralyzing manifestations, and in many cases, a lack of desire to change anything at all. The fear of eliminating guaranteed lifetime employment is quite natural; anyone can see how this might be bothersome to those with it. Understanding, however, as suggested in opening quote, is the calming agent of misunderstanding and subsequent fear. Being open to change means transitioning from inadequacy of true information to sufficiency in knowledge. This is accomplished through understanding.

Another less obvious manifestation of fear is passive-aggressive behavior, defined by Wikipedia as behavior that expresses aggression in an indirect, passive way. This includes procrastination, hostile jokes, stubbornness, resentment, sullenness, or deliberate/

repeated failure to accomplish requested tasks for which one is (often explicitly) responsible. Following is an example:

In one college of a major tier-one research university, there exists a full tenured professor who is also an associate dean. By any definition this individual is fully guaranteed a job for life. This particular college is shadowed by its larger, considerably more prominent, sibling college. Many collaborative relationships have been established between the two colleges.

The individual mentioned above, fears he would never have obtained tenure as a full professor in this larger college, and certainly would not have been fortunate enough to be an associate dean. Quite honestly, he is correct. At present, this individual is a big fish in a very small pond, as the saying goes. Through passive-aggressive behavior, this associate dean works to undue past collaborations, kill new ones, and in general create hot stick-pokes to the more prominent college. All of this is very Machiavellian in nature. On the surface, this individual promotes collaboration, but underneath, he makes every attempt to kill any attempts at collaboration. This behavior is entirely premised on fear. The fear is the loss of power or position should the lesser college ever be merged or taken over by the bigger one. Instead of looking at the potential for significant synergistic opportunities for students, the colleges, university, and the taxpayers, personal fear guides his actions.

In the book, *Love Works* by Joel Manby, the author discusses the concept of leading with love. He defines this concept with the following:

> ...we use love to define our leadership culture at Herschend Family Entertainment. Not love the emotion, but love the verb. We train our leaders to love each other, knowing that if they create enthusiasm with their employees, the employees will in turn create an enthusiastic guest experience. I think most organizations avoid discussions about how people should treat each other, and I think that's what is wrong about a lot of organizations (13).

This is the goal of our higher education institutions, and if it is not yet, for the sake of taxpayers, students, and staff as well as faculty, it should be.

CHAPTER 3

Truth #3: Tenure as a Closed System: Coercion, Groupthink, Bias and Inherently Discriminatory

Of all the ills of tenure, this last ill is the most blatant, widely recognized, tolerated and hurtful.

Guaranteed lifetime employment, a.k.a. tenure, is a closed system. As such, it promotes groupthink, capitalizes on coercion among lesser-seniority associate professors, and openly invites a natural bias and subsequent prejudice. The tenure process itself is documented to be biased, prejudicial, and inherently discriminatory. To better understand the logic of this statement, we will discuss those aspects which are impacted by the tenure model.

A friend recently attended a one-day symposium on faculty hiring of females and underrepresented minorities. The focus was on the built-in prejudice of current faculty search-and-screen committees. All associate deans, department heads, dean leadership teams, and deans themselves were invited to participate. During the workshop, Dr. Daryl Smith of Claremont Graduate University spoke extensively about national issues of the built-in prejudice of search-and-screen committees. She discussed the manifestation of this today. This is seen in ratios of females and underrepresented minorities on tenure track or as tenured faculty. Dr. Smith presented study after study on this most obvious national issue. One study showed how names alone influenced whether the committee thought a candidate was qualified or not. In that study, black sounding names were rated routinely lower for comparable qualifications versus candidates with white sounding names.

Dr. Smith produced Probity university-specific numbers, reflecting below national averages across the board. She made an adamant point to suggest "**…tenure was broken… from every perspective – theoretical, practical, moral, and ethical, the tenure process and those participating in it are exercising prejudice and bias in their decision making…**"

In a campus newspaper article, interim vice provost for faculty affairs addressed the biases and discriminatory practices of the tenure process. Her premise was solidly founded in the number of females and underrepresented minorities [not] put forth as candidates for tenured positions and faculty searches. Provost Douglas stated,

...this type of discrimination in hiring and promotion extends to our own community. At Probity, 87 percent of tenured professors are male... there's well-documented evidence of biases in the processes of hiring and promotion... most of our hiring isn't blind. Hiring is supposed to be a merit process (2).

Quantitative and Qualitative Elements of Decision Making

Decision making can be discussed in terms of both a quantitative and a qualitative process. The literature on both is nearly insurmountable. Searching Amazon for books about "decision making" returns nearly one quarter of a billion hits – that's a lot of literature on any subject!

The intent in this section is not necessarily to discuss tools and techniques for making good decisions, but instead, to lay a foundation for understanding the approaches to making better, more informed decisions.

The quantitative discipline for making better decisions is referred to as *management science*. Management science is an approach to decision making that makes extensive use of quantitative analysis according to authors David R. Anderson, Dennis J. Sweeney, Thomas A. Williams, Jeffrey D. Camm, and R. Kipp Martin, in their book entitled "An Introduction to Management Science: Quantitative Approaches to Decision Making". In addition to *management science* another widely accepted name is *operations research*. Many use these terms interchangeably. The scientific management revolution of the early 1900s, initiated by Frederick W. Taylor, provided the foundation for MS/OR.

Modern management science/operations research is generally considered to have originated during the World War II period. During that time, teams were formed to deal with strategic and tactical problems faced by the military. These teams, often consisting of people with diverse specialties (e.g., mathematicians, engineers, and behavioral scientists), were grouped together to solve a common problem via the scientific method. After the war, many of these team members continued their research on quantitative approaches to decision making.

Two developments that occurred during the post-World War II period led to the growth and use of management science in nonmilitary applications. First, continued research on quantitative approaches to decision making resulted in numerous methodological developments. Probably the most significant development was the discovery by George Dantzig in 1947, of the Simplex Method for solving linear programming problems. Many more methodological developments followed, and in 1957, the first book on operations research was published by C. W. Churchman, R. L. Ackoff, and L. E. Amoff.

Concurrently with these methodological developments, there was a virtual explosion in computing power made available through digital computers. Computers enabled practitioners to use the methodological advances to

TRUTH #3: TENURE AS A CLOSED SYSTEM: COERCION...

successfully solve a large variety of problems. The computer technology explosion continues; personal computers are now more powerful than the mainframe computers of the 1970s. Today, variants of the post-World War II methodological developments are being used on personal computers to solve problems larger than those solved on mainframe computers in the 1980s.

Problem solving can be defined as the process of identifying a difference between the actual and the desired state of affairs and then taking action to resolve the difference. For problems important enough to justify the time and effort of careful analysis, the problem-solving process involves the following seven steps:

- Identify and define the problem.
- Define the set of alternative solutions.
- Define the criterion or criteria that will be used to evaluate the alternatives.
- Evaluate the alternatives.
- Choose an alternative.
- Implement the selected alternative.
- Evaluate the results, and determine if a satisfactory solution has been obtained.

Decision making is the term generally associated with the first five steps of the problem-solving process. Thus, the first step of decision making is to identify and define the problem. Decision making ends with the choosing of an alternative, which is the act of making the decision.

Quantitative analysis truly provides a framework to evaluate selected alternatives based on sound rational and methodical thought processes. The management science approach is taught in colleges and universities around the world and usually involves one or more semesters of study.

On the qualitative side of the decision-making discussion, there is probably nothing more read in recent times than the work by Daniel Goleman entitled *Emotional Intelligence*. Emotional intelligence (EI) has been researched and reported on as the foundation from which solid, thoughtful decisions are made. In Goleman, Boyatzis, and McKee's book, *Primal Leadership*, the authors discuss the four dimensions of emotional intelligence and the six styles of leadership (3). Within the four dimensions of emotional intelligence (self-awareness, self-management, social awareness, and relationships management), there are eighteen competencies. These competencies are the vehicles of primal leadership. Even the most outstanding leader will not have all competencies. Effective leaders, though, exhibit at least one competency from each of the domains.

The four domains and their competencies, from Goleman's *Emotional Intelligence* (3–10), are listed below:

Self-Awareness

- Emotional self-awareness: Reading one's own emotions, recognizing their impact, and using "gut sense" to guide decisions.

- Accurate self-assessment: Knowing one's strengths and limits.
- Self-confidence: A sound sense of one's self-worth and capabilities.

Self-Management

- Emotional self-control: Keeping disruptive emotions and impulses under control.
- Transparency: Displaying honesty, integrity, and trustworthiness.
- Adaptability: Flexibility in adapting to changing situations or overcoming obstacles.
- Achievement: The drive to improve performance to meet inner standards of excellence.
- Initiative: Readiness to act and seize opportunities.
- Optimism: Seeing the upside in events.

Social Awareness

- Empathy: Sensing others' emotions, understanding their perspective, and taking active interest in their concerns.
- Organizational awareness: Reading the currents, decision networks, and politics at the organizational level.
- Service: Recognizing and meeting follower, client, or customer needs.

Relationship Management

- Inspirational leadership: Guiding and motivating with a compelling vision.
- Influence: Wielding a range of tactics for persuasion.
- Developing others: Bolstering others' abilities through feedback and guidance.
- Change catalyst: Initiating, managing, and leading in new directions.
- Building bonds: Cultivating and maintaining relationship webs.
- Teamwork and collaboration: Cooperation and team building.

The best, most effective leaders act according to one or more of six distinct approaches to leadership. Four of the styles – visionary, coaching, affiliative, and democratic –creates the kind of resonance that boosts performance. The other two – pacesetting and commanding – should be applied with caution.

The Six Styles of Leadership

Visionary. The visionary leader articulates where a group is going, but not how it gets there, setting people free to innovate, experiment, and take calculated risks. Inspirational leadership is the EI competence that most strongly undergirds the visionary style. Transparency, another EI competency, is also crucial. If a leader's vision is disingenuous, people sense it. The EI competency that matters most to visionary leadership, however, is empathy. The ability to sense what others feel, and understand their perspectives, helps a leader articulate a truly inspirational vision.

Coaching. The coaching style is really the art of the one-on-one. Coaches help people identify their unique strengths and weaknesses, tying those to their personal and career aspirations. Effective coaching exemplifies the EI competency of developing others, letting a leader act as a counselor. It works hand in hand with two other competencies: emotional awareness and empathy.

Affiliative. The affiliative style of leadership represents the collaborative competency in action. An affiliative leader is most concerned with promoting harmony and fostering friendly interactions. When leaders are being affiliative, they focus on the emotional needs of workers, using empathy. Many leaders who use the affiliative approach combine it with the visionary approach. Visionary leaders state a mission, set standards, and let people know whether their work is furthering group goals. Ally that with the caring approach of the affiliative leader and you have a potent combination.

Democratic. A democratic leader builds on a triad of EI abilities: teamwork and collaboration, conflict management, and influence. Democratic leaders are great listeners and true collaborators. They know how to quell conflict and create harmony. Empathy also plays a role. A democratic approach works best when as a leader, you are unsure what direction to take and need ideas from able employees. For example, IBM's Louis Gerstner, was a computer industry outsider when he became CEO of the ailing giant. He relied on seasoned colleagues for advice.

Pacesetting. Pacesetting as a leadership style must be applied sparingly, restricted to settings where it truly works. Common wisdom holds that pacesetting is admirable. The leader holds and exemplifies high standards for performance. He or she is obsessive about doing things better and faster, quickly pinpointing poor performers. Unfortunately, applied excessively, pacesetting can backfire and lead to low morale as workers think they are being pushed too hard or that the leader doesn't trust them to get their job done. The EI foundation of a pacesetter is the drive to achieve through improved performance and the initiative to seize opportunities. But a pacesetter who lacks empathy can easily be blinded to the pain of those who achieve what the leader demands. Pacesetting works best when combined with the passion of the visionary style and the team building of the affiliate style.

Commanding. The command leader demands immediate compliance with orders, but doesn't bother to explain the reasons. If subordinates fail to follow orders, these leaders resort to threats. They also seek tight control and monitoring. Of all the leadership styles, the commanding approach is the least effective. Consider what the style does to an organization's climate. Given that emotional contagion spreads most readily from the top down, an intimidating, cold leader contaminates everyone's mood. Such a leader erodes people's spirits and the pride and satisfaction they take in their work. The commanding style works in limited circumstances, and only when used judiciously. For example, in a genuine emergency, such as an approaching hurricane or a hostile take-over attempt, a take-control style can help everyone through the crisis. An effective execution of the commanding style draws on three EI competencies: influence, achievement, and initiative. In addition, self-awareness, emotional self-control, and empathy are crucial to keep the commanding style from going off track.

The literature on decision making is significant. The number of books on quantitative to qualitative foundational skills is proliferate. The discussion on decision making very naturally progresses into a discussion on leadership traits and/or characteristics themselves. It's hard to not make mention of leadership when talking about decision making. The very essence of leadership, and management for that matter, is premised on characteristics of qualitative descent.

As stated in the beginning of this section, it isn't the intent of this section to go any further with this discussion than to heighten awareness to the basic elements of effective decision making. Understanding the tools, techniques, and methodologies in practice can be further understood once the reader better acquaints himself or herself with the information above.

Business Case for Diversity and Inclusivity: It's All about Growth

A number of years back, most employees in business and industry were required to attend what was then referred to as diversity training. Diversity training, in almost every case, was one of the most boring discussions we could have. It centered on the legal aspects of being sued for discrimination in the workplace. The topic was frequently presented by human resources or the legal department. Nobody wanted to go; there was absolutely nothing positive about the training, and from year to year it never really changed.

The problem with that previous training was that it never answered the fundamental question of what benefits accrue the organization from thinking from a diverse perspective, or even valuing inclusivity (a term not then known or used). Company performance and profitability were tied to legal implications from lawsuits. Most of us at the time knew there had to be a better way to express the value of diversity in the workforce other than just to avoid litigation, after all we are all human beings with something to contribute. We desperately wanted a concept or model we could sell that resonated with each employee.

Then, around the late 1990s, the concept of diversity in the workforce took a decidedly different turn. We began talking about diversity as more than simply a race or gender issue and started looking at it as an array of diverse characteristics representative of the general employee population. The familiar things associated with age, race, gender, religion, physical ability/disability, and national ethnicity were still identified, as they should be, but additional characteristics (as depicted) such as family situation, sexual orientation, veteran status, language spoken, work experience, education, thought, geographical location, functional discipline, and international experience all came into the fold, contributing toward a more complete perspective of diversity in the workplace.

TRUTH #3: TENURE AS A CLOSED SYSTEM: COERCION...

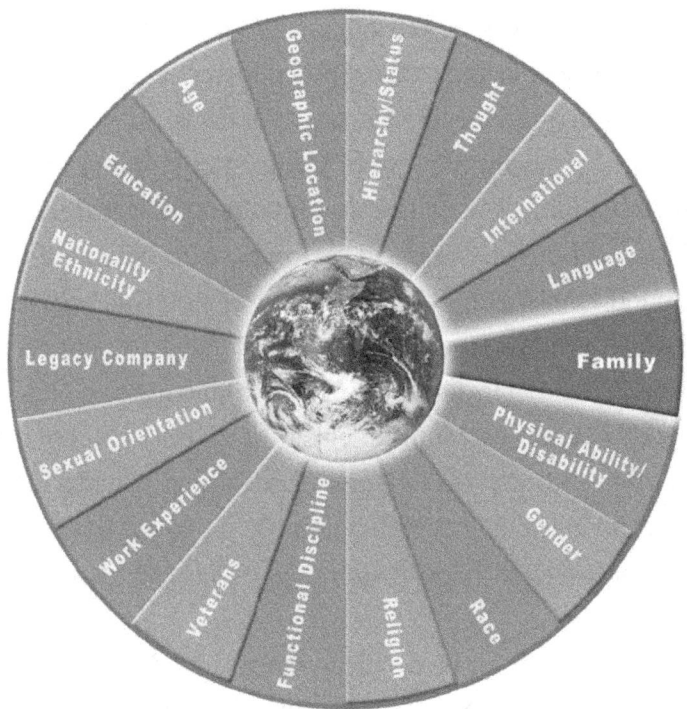

FIGURE 3.1

The identification of these additional characteristics also ushered in new presentation material with a different slant. Now we talked about:

- diversity being an imperative for business survival
- diverse teams making better decisions and better decisions making us more competitive
- creating an atmosphere that helped great ideas to thrive
- celebrating our uniqueness

During this time, we also began talking about creating an inclusive culture as well as metrics for measuring such.

Strategic objectives were being created in most every organization. These objectives talked about hiring and promoting at all levels; recognizing, developing, and using diverse employee talent; increasing the use of mentoring; building relationships and alliances with local communities and highly diverse colleges and universities; and building a bidirectional line of open and honest communication. All of this was backed by numerous programs and initiatives intended to support the stated strategic objectives. Things were starting to solidify in terms of actions and commitments. The entirety of all of these things was years beyond our previous training. We had moved away from compliance-related training into logical reasoning attendant to increasing growth in our organizations.

During this same time, a video emerged by Joel Barker entitled, "Wealth, Innovation and Diversity", which explicitly depicted why we should value diversity in our organizations. Barker presented something comparable to the figure below.

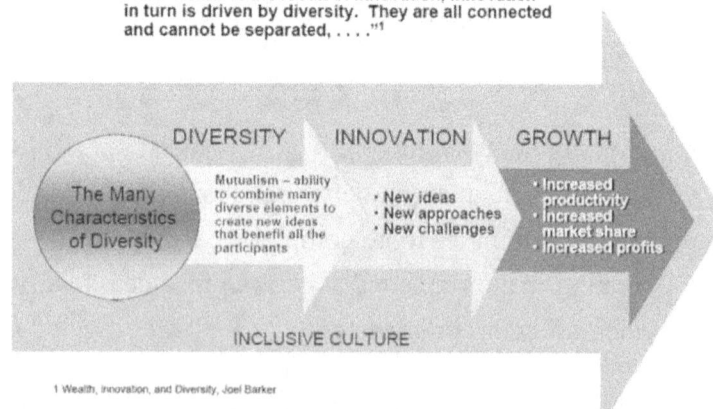

FIGURE 3.2

TRUTH #3: TENURE AS A CLOSED SYSTEM: COERCION...

In this video, Barker says the following:

> Now it is time to begin to connect wealth, innovation, and diversity more clearly. We've seen how diversity sets the stage for new ideas and how mutualism manifests those ideas into new combinations. Another way to describe these new ideas is as innovations. And successful innovations add new value to the world. New value creates new wealth. And, according to the Economist magazine, as much as 40 percent of all the increased wealth in the world each year comes from innovation. So ongoing innovation enlarges the economic pie from which the whole world can dine. While there are several kinds of innovations, I have found that one kind in particular adds the most new value and the most new wealth. I have labeled these "paradigm-shifting" innovations.

What Barker refers to as "paradigm-shifting" innovations, are more generally discussed as "disruptive technologies." Disruptive technologies are those technologies that exist in the gaps of pure disciplines, at the intersection of the brilliance of pure disciplines. In this scenario, disruptive technologies require the recognition of the value of other disciplines – one of our diversity characteristics.

Around 1999, I remember attending an NAACP luncheon in downtown Fort Wayne, Indiana. It was intended to provide yet additional insight into the value of diversity. While the session itself wasn't as detailed as that presented above, it did stir my emotions. I remember halfway through the session getting up and making a phone call to my boss, saying that I wanted to start a diversity council in our company. His comment, being always open to new initiatives, was, "Go ahead and do it; sounds great to me." After returning to the office, I did just that. I pulled the demographics from our facility and selected quantities of individuals to be representatives for our diversity council. In staying with our philosophy that diversity was more than compliance characteristics, I selected representation from as many of the multitude of diverse characteristics as I could find. I really wasn't sure what to expect. I remember pulling together our first collection of individuals called the diversity council. One of the first questions I was asked in that opening session was, "Isn't diversity supposed to be gender and race predominantly?" I knew right then and there if our own group possessed a lack of understanding and couldn't differentiate between diversity as we defined it and compliance characteristics, the general population was certainly going to be confused.

To help the general employee population better understand what we meant by diversity, we would take each diversity-related characteristic and do an entire sixteen-foot-wide by nine-foot-tall display every other month. The displays received a lot of attention. In fact, the displays received so much attention that other businesses within our overall company began borrowing our displays for their facilities. Over the years, our diversity council changed personnel, as most time spent was voluntary, but the passion was always there. I really believe we got it, and it was our purpose in life to help others better understand it. We never meant to change people's minds on a given diverse characteristic, only to heighten their awareness to all aspects of that characteristic in hopes they would develop a more open mind to differences. Having grown up in a very diverse neighborhood as a child, I never really felt animosity against an entire diverse characteristic, but that wasn't to say I didn't like certain people, whether they be mean, rude, or obnoxious.

Interestingly enough, the generations of people we call "Generation X" and "Generation Y (Millennials)" really do get it. They are the most accepting of differences in people. In fact, most in these two cohort groups don't see any value in even discussing varying diversity characteristics. They simply already accept these many differences. In fact, as I go around the country doing generational awareness presentations, I routinely hear stories that are indicative of how open these cohorts are to diversity of every kind. At no time has anyone in either of these two groups led me to believe they would even waste one minute on gender, race, or ethnicity discussions. They take it for granted that people from all diverse groups are their friends, colleagues, parents, or grandparents. Inclusivity and acceptance of diversity is their norm, as I hope someday will be the case for all human beings; especially those participating in the tenure process.

Closed Versus Open Systems

Seeing the bigger picture is very similar to the concept of open versus closed systems. In a closed system, the organization or unit only sees within itself, whereas in an open system, the organization takes into consideration the external environment. In the open system, the organization considers the multitude of outside factors that have an influence on the organization, from environmental to competition with other similar organizations within a given industry.

Reviewing the example provided in the introduction:

> ...to become tenured, a non-tenured faculty member must serve a life of silence against perceived challenges to faculty and tenure, servitude to those full professors who have direct influence over the non-tenured fate, and collusion against those who pose a challenge to the status quo. Once a non-tenured faculty member has served their seven years of servitude, they are voted on by their faculty superiors for acceptability into the tenured ranks. The process is extremely subjective, frequently leaning to the loudest among those with voting privileges, and in the end may be determined simply by what is termed "collegiality" or "non-collegiality". In other words, did they like you?

Again, as Van Alstyne makes point of in his book, *Freedom and Tenure in the Academy*:

> The observation offered in this critique is that the installation, promotion, and "tenuring" of

only those satisfying only such criteria as characterize the incumbent faculty's judgments – of what counts as "relevant" work and what counts in being a "competent" candidate – make the system self-sealing (literally self-proving of its own criteria) [inward looking and potentially discriminatory]. The incumbent faculty was itself selected and advanced by prevailing notions of "relevance" of subject matter interest and prevailing notions of "competence" to do suitable work. Accordingly, succeeding generation of faculty may tend to be quite indistinguishable from the last generation. The structure of the system itself thus makes it more or less impervious to change (IX).

Essentially, the individuals who make up the system itself are by definition the very individuals who make the decision on potentially new, tenured faculty. A system that is self-contained is by definition a closed system and by Van Alstyne's definition, "**…succeeding generation of faculty may tend to be quite indistinguishable from the last generation…**"

It is this aspect of a closed system, e.g. the tenure system, which creates a subconscious element of bias and prejudice. Most literature on this topic suggests it may not even be a conscious consideration, although it may be. It may simply be under the umbrella of "collegiality" or "lack of collegiality"; the easiest manner to discard someone not liked, or, perhaps not like the voting individuals of the tenure committee.

How the Tenure Process Contributes to Coercion, Groupthink and Prejudice

Coercion ...is the practice of forcing another party to act in an involuntary manner (whether through action or inaction) by use of threats or intimidation or some other form of pressure or force, and describes a set of various, different, yet similar types of forceful actions that violate the free will of an individual to induce a desired response. These actions can include, but are not limited to, extortion, blackmail, torture, and threats to induce favors. In law, coercion is codified as a duress crime. Such actions are used as leverage to force the victim to act in a way contrary to their own interests. Coercion may involve the actual infliction of physical pain/injury or psychological harm in order to enhance the credibility of a threat. The threat of further harm may lead to the cooperation or obedience of the person being coerced (Wikipedia).

"...In law, coercion is codified as a duress crime..." – Who would push this issue from within the tenure committee? Certainly not the associate professors who wish to be promoted to full professors someday!

Perhaps the best way to present this section is to provide a real-life example. Assume an assistant professor wishes to go

TRUTH #3: TENURE AS A CLOSED SYSTEM: COERCION...

before the departmental tenure committee to ask for a promotion into the rank of associate professor, which comes with the much sought after guaranteed lifetime employment (tenure). The committee, in this scenario, is made up of tenured faculty who are both associate and full professors. These associate and full professors will be the ones voting on whether the assistant professor will be granted associate professor status and therefore receive guaranteed lifetime employment. Keep in mind the above discussion where "...to become tenured, a non-tenured faculty member must serve a life of silence against perceived challenges to faculty and tenure, servitude to those full professors who have direct influence over the non-tenured fate, and collusion against those who pose a challenge to the status quo..."

In the voting, departmental, faculty tenure committee, there is the mix of associate and full professors. The voting associate professors know that someday they will have to go before the full professors to be voted on for promotion into full professor rank. Moving from associate to full professor means an increase in salary and therefore higher annual incremental pay increases for time-in-position.

During the tenure committee discussion on whether an assistant professor should be allowed into the associate professor rank and subsequently given guaranteed lifetime employment, the full professor will make their opinions known, sometimes quite vocally. The full professors will then ask what, if any, opposition to their opinions might exist; this because everyone is allowed to have an opinion and to voice it.

What happens, however, is as expected; not one of the associate professors speak out differently than the voices of the full professors. Why, might one ask? The answer is, to do so would potentially harm the associate professor's chance for full professor when their time comes around. The tenured associate professors know this and the full professors know this; nothing more need be said. This is coercion by its very definition and is a crime, which should be punishable by law.

Groupthink is a psychological phenomenon that occurs within a group of people, in which the desire for harmony or conformity in the group results in an incorrect or deviant decision-making outcome. Group members try to minimize conflict and reach a consensus decision without critical evaluation of alternative ideas or viewpoints, and by isolating themselves from outside influences.

Loyalty to the group requires individuals to avoid raising controversial issues or alternative solutions, and there is loss of individual creativity, uniqueness, and independent thinking. Through groupthink, the dysfunctional group dynamics of the "in group" produces an "illusion of invulnerability" (an inflated certainty that the right decision has been made). Thus the "in group" significantly overrates their own abilities in decision-making, and significantly underrates the abilities of their opponents (the "out group").

Antecedent factors such as group cohesiveness, faulty group structure, and situational context (e.g., community panic) play into the likelihood of whether or not groupthink will impact the decision-making process.

Groupthink is a construct of social psychology, but has an extensive reach and influences literature in the fields of communication studies, political science, management, and organizational theory, as well as important aspects of deviant religious cult behavior – (Wikipedia).

Whether coercion or groupthink is in play, it is easy to see how a closed system promotes a single-minded outcome. This outcome can directly result in bias and prejudice against those who do not meet the identity of the voting group; and most likely will result in a "no" vote based on "collegiality" or some other subjective determination of qualification.

Microinequity refers to the ways in which individuals are "either singled out or overlooked, ignored, or otherwise discounted" based on an unchangeable characteristic such as race or gender. A microinequity generally takes the form of a gesture, different kind of language, treatment, or even tone of voice. It is suggested that the perceptions that cause the manifestation of microinequities are deeply rooted and unconscious. The cumulative effect of microinequities can impair a person's performance in the workplace or classroom, damage self-esteem, and may eventually lead to that person's withdrawal from the situation.

In the original articles on this subject in the 1970s, Mary Rowe defined microinequities as "apparently small events which are often ephemeral and hard to prove – events which are covert, often unintentional, frequently unrecognized by the perpetrator, which occur wherever people are perceived to be 'different.'"

There is a difference between the concepts of "inequality" and "inequity." An inequality implies there is some comparison being made. For example, if your boss doesn't listen attentively to you, that in and of itself is not a microinequality; however, if your boss listens attentively to all of your co-workers, but not to you, that might be a microinequality.

An inequity, by contrast, is simply something (that may be perceived to be) unfair or unjust under the circumstances. Thus a micro-inequity may occur with only one person on the scene, if that person is treated in an unfair or unjust manner. (Of course it is possible and even likely that many micro-inequities support or lead to an unequal environment for people of a given group; but the two concepts are different.) (Wikipedia).

Prejudice is an irrational and inflexible opinion, formed on the basis of limited and insufficient knowledge. Stereotypes, often give rise to prejudice. Exposure to exaggerated and rigid images of a particular group might lead us to prejudge anyone we identify with that group (Bucher 71).

> ...more often than not, talk about prejudice focuses on "them" rather than "us". Many of us can readily sense prejudice in others, but seeing it in ourselves is a challenge. When someone mentions the word prejudice, what comes to mind? Is prejudice something ordinary or extraordinary? Do prejudiced people look and act like you? It is important to understand that we learn prejudice just like any other subject at school. The lyrics of a song from the Broadway musical South Pacific tell us that the learning process starts very early in life. "...you've got to be taught before it's too late, before you are 6 or 7 or 8, to hate all the people your relatives hate." Research indicates that children as young as 4 or 5 years of age begin to show signs of prejudice. We are more apt to simply believe what we hear. By the time we are adults, prejudging people for whatever reason can be almost an unconscious habit. Additionally, prejudice offers us a quick

and easy way to categorize all the new and different people we meet each day. It takes much more time and effort to withhold judgment until we really know someone (Bucher 72).

The unconscious mind of the individuals in a closed tenure system can and may, very naturally, extend their beliefs, biases, and prejudices against those who are not like them. This can contribute directly to the lack of "different" genders and underrepresented minorities in the tenured ranks of the academy. While it is easy as a voting member to suggest otherwise, the data suggests this may be true. Revisiting Van Alstyne's earlier words, a system that is self-contained is by definition a closed system and "…succeeding generation of faculty may tend to be quite indistinguishable from the last generation…"

Similar (also great) minds think alike, is how the saying goes. **In this scenario, similar minds in a closed system, through microinequities and preconceived biases, and subsequently through the crime of coercion and the psychological phenomenon of groupthink, clearly provide the opportunity and apparent realities of discrimination.** The tenure process is broke from this perspective.

CHAPTER 4

Addressing Those Questions Which are the Essence of the Argument

As we've moved from one survey to the next, from one study to the next, from one article to the next and from one book to the next, there are a few very basic defenses used by those who wish most desperately to keep tenure in place as is, or with only minimal modification. The topics that follow address the predominance of those who wish to maintain guaranteed lifetime employment.

How Do We Attract the Best and Brightest?

This question is premised on the idea it is only through guaranteed lifetime employment that colleges and universities can attract and retain the best and the brightest; short of this there is no other way to attract these elite individuals.

What do Apple Computer, Nike, Microsoft, Samsung, Starbucks, and Facebook all have in common? They are just a few of the 50 most innovative companies in the world in 2014. What do Comcast, EBay, Mattel, Home Depot, MasterCard, and News Corp all have in common? They are just a few of the top performing United States companies listed in 2014. What do Mars (maker of M&Ms), Google, Boston Consulting Group, Qualcomm, DreamWorks, and Intuit all have in common? They are just a few of the top 100 best companies to work for as reported in 2014. **Surprisingly enough, none of these companies, the most innovative, top performing, or best companies to work for, offer guaranteed lifetime employment – none of them!**

Interestingly as well, not one of these companies has a problem recruiting their share of the best and the brightest employees; again without offering guaranteed lifetime employment. Their challenge is not getting their fair share of the best and the brightest; it is finding enough qualified individuals with the right skills to perform the many additional tasks of their organizations. There is a difference. Just as was previously discussed with manufacturing, production is running at pre-recession levels with a third less people, yet manufacturing as an industry is woefully short of skilled labor. They are not looking for the best and brightest, just those qualified to perform in the new high-tech manufacturing industry. The best and brightest are very few of the many employees our organizations require to hire. In fact, no organization, if they did hire only the best and brightest, could even remotely hope to retain such a high-end staff of people. Truth being, there are levels of players, and all are necessary to run an organization.

Let's say that as a program manager in business and industry, upon award of a new program, you ask for 25 of the best and brightest employees the company has on staff. Why? Because as a program manager you feel your program is the most important program in the company, with unending upward potential and significant revenue to be gained over its many theoretical years of life. The truth is, however, you don't really need 25 of the best and the brightest. Why? Because you don't have enough of the type of work that would keep 25 of the best and brightest engaged and content. In actuality, what you get, and what you need, are 1-3 of the best and brightest, 20 who are people who can get things done and may even be considered "B" players, and then of course, you will be given a couple who, in your opinion, should have been let go years earlier. It takes this combination of talent to successfully run a program within cost, schedule, and performance requirements set forth by the customer.

Great companies, whether they be the most innovative, the top performing, or the best companies to work for, attract top talent. Why? Because top talent migrates to these companies. Top talent wants to go where there is challenging work and an opportunity to change the world through their efforts.

Naomi Riley wrote an article for the *Wall Street Journal* detailing the success of W. Olin College of Engineering in attracting 140 applicants for every faculty position. This is without offering tenure and with the applicants knowing they can be fired.

> November 20, 2010 – Needham, Mass. When Richard Miller told his colleagues that he was leaving his tenured position as dean of the University of Iowa's engineering school, a number of them asked if he was smoking dope. Mr. Miller was stepping down to become the first president of the Franklin W. Olin College of Engineering in Massachusetts – and Olin, which opened its doors 10 years ago, does not offer tenure to its faculty.
>
> "Don't you realize that if you go there you'll never work in higher education again?" Mr. Miller recalls his friends asking. "They'll think you turned in your union card—that you don't care about the core values of academic freedom." Mr. Miller, a jovial man who now presides over a campus of 350 students in this suburb west of Boston, says he didn't care. Having tenure is like being placed in "golden handcuffs," he told me. "There are more important things than permanent employment" – like offering students a fulfilling education.
>
> One wishes that other academics shared his opinion. In the meantime, Olin is showing

what's possible when a school sheds tenure, one of the most antiquated and counterproductive employment policies in the American economy. Instituted at a time when people in most professions remained in the same job for life, tenure today is an economic anomaly. The policy protects laziness and incompetence, and rewards often-obscure research rather than good teaching.

[Olin] is ranked 8th in undergraduate engineering by U.S. News and World Report.

Though Olin doesn't offer lifetime employment, the school's vision has been appealing enough to attract an average of 140 applicants for every faculty position. In all but three cases, Olin got its top choice to fill each teaching slot.

Mark Somerville left a tenure-track position in the physics department at Vassar to teach at Olin. "It was not a hard decision to make," he says. Mr. Somerville says he has found that the lack of tenure has changed his teaching and research interests for the better.

"When one is on the tenure track," he says, "the clock is ticking. There is a certain day on which you will have to produce a stack of papers." He's no longer worried about publishing a certain amount by a particular date. Instead, he's free to pursue research he finds interesting – something Mr. Somerville says has been "liberating."

The passion of the Olin faculty and students is unmistakable. Mr. Miller calls them "a community of zealots" – not exactly what you expect from a bunch of engineers. But then giving up tenure seems to do some strange things to people (3).

The Center for College Affordability and Productivity (CCAP) discusses this point in their paper "25 Ways to Reduce the Cost of College."

> …Some proponents suggest that the lifetime job security provided by academic tenure is required to attract quality faculty members to the professorate. Those making this argument assume that the extensive training period necessary to obtain a Ph.D. qualification, in addition to the long probationary period, would deter many academically capable individuals from aspiring to become professors if lifetime job security was not available…
>
> The case has been made that tenure is cost-effective based on the assumption that most scholars are risk averse and are willing to accept lower pay for job security, suggesting that

academics forego higher salaries by working at a college, and that the job security offered by tenure is compensation for a lower salary than they might otherwise receive. The evidence suggests the opposite is true–that tenure is not a cost-effective employment instrument...

An increasing number of non-tenured, full-time faculty work for lower wages than their tenured and tenure-track counterparts, indicating that colleges can and do cost-effectively attract qualified faculty without the job security provided by tenure...

The current tenure process requires new hires on the tenure-track to serve a probationary period of up to seven years before they are eligible to receive tenure. At the conclusion of the probationary period, faculty members are evaluated based on their supposed merits in teaching, research, and service. The assumption is that faculty members who have proven their worth will continue to perform well for the remainder of their careers and this therefore merits a lifetime employment contract... [this is no more true in academics than it is in business/industry]" (15-17).

Those that argue in public higher education that any given college or university can't recruit top talent without offering guaranteed lifetime employment are oblivious to what's going on in the "real-world". **If you offer something great, then you will get great people who want to be part of it.** If you offer mediocre curriculums or courses, then that's what you will get as talent. To suggest that a college or university has to offer guaranteed lifetime employment to someone to entice them to come screams that the college or university has nothing better to offer. It cannot be argued that there are only a few top talents who can teach mathematics or liberal arts; that we disproved above when discussing the oversupply of highly educated PhD/doctoral talent who can't find jobs because the more senior among tenured faculty refuse to move on into retirement, even at age 65, 70, 75, 80, and above. Colleges and universities, just like business and industry, do not need to hire one hundred percent of the top talent any more than those companies listed above.

This brings to the surface another truth in business and industry from which colleges and universities would benefit. No organization can be everything to everyone! The parallel to this is, no college or university can, or perhaps more applicably, should be everything to everyone. Most institutions are unrealistically striving to be all things to all people in their quest for students, reputation, and support rather than focusing their resources on the mission and programs that they can accomplish with distinction (Dickeson 15).

Colleges and universities certainly do have very specific niches for which they are well known and respected. However, most colleges and universities offer a broad array of other non-niche specific courses and curriculums in which they also offer guaranteed lifetime employment. *If a college or university is preeminent in what they offer, they will undoubtedly gain preeminent faculty to work with them.* Apple does not have this problem. Apple Computer offers preeminent products and great people flock to their doorsteps. If you are the best in the world at the products or services you provide, then you will never have to offer guaranteed lifetime employment to those wishing to be part of your great organization.

Dr. Adams, an extremely intelligent man with great vision. He is the Dean of a College. During his interview process, he made numerous arguments that education as a term and concept was not well understood by students or their parents. Recognizing the college was experiencing dwindling enrollments and the student quality indicators trailed most of the rest of the university, he launched an aggressive effort to make the college preeminent in all they offered. His argument was if the College was preeminent in everything they offered, students and their parents would flock in mass to the college's doors trying to get in. This in turn would provide higher student quality indicators to choose from. The key, according to Dr. Adams, was to offer a better product and you will attract a better student and larger quantities of students. Below are highlights from the "College Strategic Plan 2019 – 2024."

> [...The College has made great strides since its creation in 1959. From our humble beginnings we have grown to be the third largest college at Probity with 10 locations around the state.

Much has been accomplished in the past years establishing the college as a national leader in education. Through this growth period, the college remains committed to quality, undergraduate education, while also cultivating a climate of excellent graduate education and impactful research. However, in some ways we are being constrained in our further development and full potential by our past, as well as the public and academic perception of what "education" is or should be. Instead, we need to step beyond this and re-define ourselves, which will lead us to be viewed as a valued discipline that has a positive impact on society.

As the nature of education evolves, so too must our college if we are to continue providing timely and relevant programs that meet the needs of employers both today and tomorrow. Education is a pervasive feature of our contemporary culture, but it is more than that; it is a defining feature of the human condition.

The uniqueness of the College is not only in its subject matter but that it is at Probity University, a research-intensive institution. In addition, the College is a large and diverse unit at Probity University ...With the resources available, including the large number of faculty, staff, and students, we need to become the leaders in defining the body of knowledge for education and find opportunities to exploit our uniqueness. We are special because we are the leaders in the definition and preparation of those who have a unique role to play in business and industry.

It is time for the College to step out of the shadows of our history and the public perceptions of "education" and start down the path to transform the College and what it means to be a student, alumni, faculty, and staff of our programs. It is time for the College to lead this nation in the definition and preparation in the 21st Century. This can be accomplished through a shared vision that goes well beyond our individual needs and the needs of any single department or program. The College has an opportunity to be the thought leader for the nation in preparing graduates that will become the engine of change necessary to revitalize and grow the economy of the state and the nation. This higher purpose and shared vision will be our focal point for everything we do and every decision we make: the definition and preparation of the 21st Century student.]

How Do We Keep People From Leaving?

The question in its full length is, "How do we keep people from leaving if we do not offer them guaranteed lifetime employment?"

This question is every Human Resource professional's concern. The answer lies in thousands of books and articles by experts from one end of the spectrum to the other. What has to be done to keep good people from leaving? The answer is multifaceted and includes such things as smart recruitment, performance feedback, training and development, career opportunities, compensation, benefits, mentoring, coaching, performance incentives, a safe working environment, and a myriad of other work-related factors. All of these characteristics have to be balanced in such a manner as to be perceived as the right combination of value to the newly hired employee. Notice, however, not in any of the above was guaranteed lifetime employment mentioned; not once! The reason being: it simply isn't necessary.

To suggest the only way to hire and retain the required talent is to blow-off what the rest of the world does daily to retain its top talent, and all other talent for that matter, is naïve and lacks maturity of understanding of how the real world works. First and foremost, *good people are always in high demand and don't need guaranteed lifetime employment to be gainfully employed.* Superiors will always look for and protect those who make them look good. This is one of the first rules of management; hire the right people. As managers and leaders, we are only as good as those around us. This is why new leaders frequently bring others with whom they have had positive experience to the newly formed team. Good people simply do not need guaranteed lifetime employment as a carrot. In fact, good people aren't working at a given organization because of miscellaneous perks. They are generally working at a given organization for other intrinsic purposes; they like the energy of change, the fast-paced opportunities, the type of research being done, and many other similar reasons. Many take positions in organizations that have lateral or lesser benefits than a previous opportunity.

Colleges and universities do not have any problems that have not already been solved in business and industry; this is not unique in this instance.

One of the top reasons cited by employees, year after year, for leaving a company has to do with the employee's supervisor. Lack of a genuine supervisor, who cares about the employee's growth and development is crucial to the individual employee feeling a sense of belonging – feeling that someone cares for him or her.

One of the many ways to keep employees is to offer a solid and applicable career development approach. The next few paragraphs address this.

There are many forms of career development models. Some models are employee driven while others are organizationally driven. Those organizationally driven models, however, are becoming fewer and fewer, heading the way of the dinosaurs.

It is important to differentiate between career development and training for a given task or job. Training is very much in the interest of a company or organization. It enhances the skills of its workforce, therefore increasing the likelihood of growing the business. Career development, however, is something much different. Career development prepares one for a career. It may include training along the way, but it is greater than simply preparing someone for the next short-term assignment. Now, one could argue that a sufficiently large number of training opportunities over a prolonged period of time might actually, by default, lead to a career development model, although it was never intended to be one. In this section, when we talk about career development models, we are talking about planned, bigger picture, coordinated and orchestrated, cohesive sets of initiatives, assignments, education, and training.

Understanding the Basic Model

At the basic level, a career development model might look like the following figure.

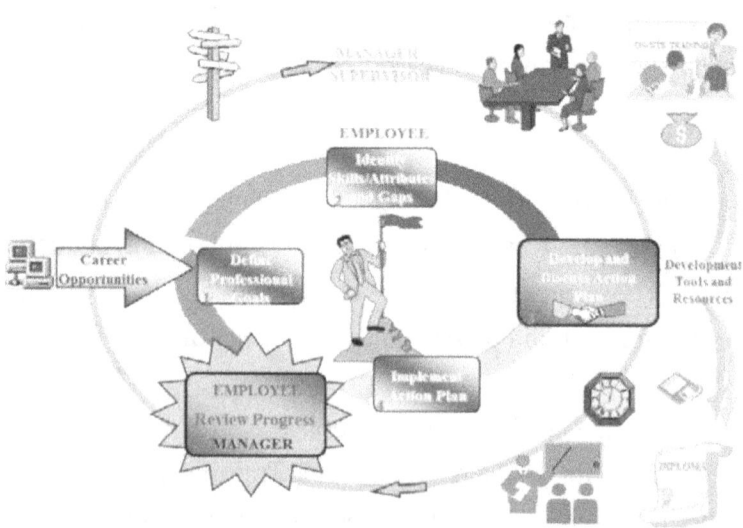

FIGURE 4.1

The model has five basic steps or phases:

- Employee defines his or her professional goals
- Employee identifies skills, attributes, and gaps
- Employee develops an action plan and then proceeds to discuss the plan with his/her supervisor
- Employee implements the action plan with the manager's approval
- Employee and manager monitor the action plan for applicability as time goes on and adequacy

In most models, how one accomplishes these five steps can be somewhat cryptic. In some cases, templates are provided, in others, words describe what could happen. In this model, we are actually going to focus on using the same process as that used in designing real-time, embedded hardware- and software-integrated computer systems; in other words, that used in rocket science.

Succession Planning as a Career Development Model

We would be remiss if we didn't address career development from a succession planning perspective. Within industry and business, the number one reason cited by people leaving the organization today and in the past two years, has been a lack of career opportunity, or more appropriately stated, a lack of known career opportunities.

Current career development takes place through one of three sources: (1) the function/discipline manager, (2) the program or work organization manager, and/or (3) the corporate-provided career development model.

In each of these three cases, the perspective of career development is focused on those aspects most applicable to the career coach, as detailed below. In common, however, is the underlying premise that each coaching opportunity is bounded by a short-term and narrowly focused perspective, therefore lacking in the breadth of the solution.

Functional managers, or discipline-specific managers, are responsible for making sure that resources are available for current and upcoming programs. To this end, they work to identify what programs – by type, size, and complexity – are forthcoming, and what skills will be required. Then, the functional managers determine which individuals with which skills will become available in time to work on the target programs.

The final step of the career matching process is to match the available supply with the future demand. From a career development perspective then, the functional manager works diligently to determine where a given individual will be placed on a continuous basis, from program to program. By virtue of the functional manager's perspective being a six- to twelve-month horizon, the career development advice is quite naturally going to be limited to this same relatively short time period. The responsibilities of the functional manager themselves are bound by perspective and time, and are generally limited in scope to program opportunities.

The program or work organization performs career development from the same short-term perspective. The program manager's perspective of work to be performed is nearly always limited to the length of his or her program, and is quite naturally bound by this fixed time period. Individual employee career development, therefore, is equally bound to this time period. And, in fact, the program manager relies on the functional/discipline manager to make career development choices outside the time bounds of the given program's duration, a hand-in-glove approach to a perceived holistic career development model.

The program manager, therefore, worries about the individual during the length of the program, while the functional manager worries about development across programs within the six- to twelve-month program-planning window.

A company may provide a third opportunity for career development, namely, self-identification, where an individual would like to be in some forward-thinking period of time. The given company-sponsored website for career development basically relinquishes the maternal/paternal responsibilities for career development by placing the burden for the future, desired position in the hands of the individual. The corporate model begins by asking the employee to visualize where she or he wants to be. This is followed up by a gap analysis, examining where the employee is now and their desired end state. The problem with this approach is the inevitable question from the individual requesting career development guidance, "What's available for me to do?"

It is this question that goes only partially answered in any of the above three provided opportunities for career development. To fully answer the question means to have a plan for succession for each and every individual in the target employee population pool. In other words, we can tell employees what they will be doing within the context of a given program (program manager), across multiple programs (functional manager), or assist them if they know where they want to end up over time. Yet here exists another perspective, that being peer-level tasks or responsibilities within or across disciplines.

Succession planning is performed for some minimal, immediate leadership positions within the organization, but the bulk of the organization lies well below these few higher-level positions. In fact, more than 90 percent of the target-exempt population falls outside most succession planning models.

Succession planning, if done properly, is a full-time, fully supported effort to determine successors in time-phase with required attendant training. At the highest level, the process is composed of identifying positions – successors who are ready now, in one to three years, three to five years, and so on – and the required next assignments, training, and education to prepare these future successors for their target positions. Although simple in theory, it clearly is exhaustively rigorous in practice. Constant updates, coupled with advancing and evaluating of development plans, require dedicated attention. Yet in the end, this practice solves one of the top reasons nearly fifty percent of the population currently leaves industry and business; they perceive no career opportunity or potential for one.

Utilizing an effective succession development model provides a clear and known career path for each individual employee and the required development to advance to those many next positions.

How Do We Ensure Faculty Can Teach as They Feel Appropriate?

This topic is one of the two underlying premises for tenure's beginnings; it is all about academic freedom – the freedom to teach and research as described in the 1940 Statement of Principles on Academic Freedom and Tenure.

Perhaps one of the best recent discussions on academic freedom is from Gary Olson in his book, *A Creature of our Own Making.*

> Academic freedom, for example, is often misunderstood to be a blanket freedom, covering any and all faculty speech and behavior. In reality, however, academic freedom allows faculty members to engage in research on controversial subjects (and, by extension, discuss those subjects in their classrooms) without fear of reprisal (4).

> It does not protect us, for example, from other types of utterances and behavior, such as slander or libel, bullying co-workers, lying on curriculum vitae, or conducting one's classes in irresponsible ways (4). Most of us in academe cherish the protections afforded by academic

freedom, but too many are unclear as to its limits. I have known colleagues who believed that academic freedom allows them to say anything they want, to anyone, in any venue, or to engage in behavior that most observers would assume to be inappropriate in any other workplace (109).

In fact, academic freedom has been claimed as an excuse for the most abusive and non-collegial behavior – shouting at colleagues, publicly berating students or staff members, defaming supervisors or other university administrators, and shirking professional duties.

Department heads have told me countless stories of how academic freedom has become the generic excuse for any number of irresponsible acts. One chair described a senior professor who missed a substantial number of her classes. When confronted with evidence of her absenteeism, she told the chair that as an academic she had the freedom to conduct her courses in any way she deemed appropriate (110).

Another department head said one of her professors managed to avoid teaching this course the entire quarter by assigning a graduate research assistant to "facilitate discussions."

I know of yet another incident in which a fistfight erupted between two colleagues at a faculty meeting, resulting in bruises and a bloody nose. Both later contended during a formal hearing that they were "covered" by academic freedom and that the university had no recourse beyond reprimanding them for disrupting an official departmental meeting.

The practice of citing academic freedom to condone a limitless range of bad behavior has begun to take on the flavor of that hackneyed student excuse: The dog ate my paper (or, nowadays, my computer crashed).

In reality, academic freedom, like tenure itself, is not a blanket protection...

The modern concept of academic freedom has two meanings. First, it refers to the right of an institution to manage its own curriculum and academic affairs without governmental interference...

The second meaning of academic freedom involved the concept that faculty members may engage in research on controversial subjects (and, by extension, discuss those subjects in their classrooms) without fear of reprisal. This refers specifically to academic subjects and is not a blanket protection for any and all speech in any venue...

> The distinction between speech related to one's discipline on the one hand, and utterances about extra-disciplinary matters on the other, is key to understanding academic freedom…

Since the age of five, I have been in school taking classes, minus a couple of years. I love learning; it comes easily to me. In all of my classes over these many years, there may have been a handful of times when a professor did not use a standard textbook – one which is generally available through any bookstore. In math, science, technology, MBA courses, psychology, philosophy, education, and all the other courses I have taken to eventually attain my Doctorate, I can count on one hand the number of professors who did not use some form of textbook. That doesn't mean a professor can't express the facts of any given socio-economic scenario, but in general, in nearly every class I have ever had, there was never an issue with what was said – unless it was a personal opinion which didn't have a place in the classroom to begin with. So perhaps I am a tad confused, or have just been lucky, but where does academic freedom come into play? Pick a textbook and teach to it. Does this act require academic freedom? Keep in mind, academic freedom was one of the two underlying premises of the 1940 Statement.

Point being, tenure, and its premise of academic freedom, is a relic of a time gone by. It has no applicability in today's environment. By the time a professor makes a point of a given social situation, the students have already heard about it through Facebook, Twitter, LinkedIn, or any number of other social mediums. I would be floored if a professor, most of which do not know how to use many of these social mediums, knew something with which today's students were not already familiar.

Two additional points to be made here: (1) every human being has the right to free speech under the First Amendment to the United States Constitution, and (2) academic freedom is no longer an issue in higher education, and if it becomes one, it can be dealt with through the courts, just like that which happens in business and industry.

The First Amendment (Amendment I) to the United States Constitution is part of the Bill of Rights that prohibits the making of any law respecting an establishment of religion, impeding the free exercise of religion, abridging the freedom of speech, infringing on the freedom of the press, interfering with the right to peaceably assemble or prohibiting the petitioning for a governmental redress of grievances (Wikipedia).

Additionally, as stated briefly above, for anyone in business and industry, this conversation most likely seems somewhat like "...seriously? Are you kidding me? ...". Again, if any individual in business or industry were to say something not representative of an organization's moral or philosophical perspective, certainly we would expect consequences, as discussed previously.

How then, given the above First Amendment and the court system, does guaranteed lifetime employment sustain itself as a defense for common sense?

How Do We Create Excellence in a Given Discipline?

The answer to this question requires another question: "How does any preeminent business or industry create excellence in their given market niche?" The answer: they focus their resources on a product or service niche they want to capture or dominate, and they hire first-rate talent.

Excellence comes from focus. Again, an organization, either in business/industry or academia, cannot, or more correctly, should not, be everything to everybody. To do so depletes resources and weakens those areas where the organizational entity could become preeminent.

Previous discussions already addressed how to attract the best and brightest and how to retain these many individuals. If given a propensity to be successful in attracting and retaining exceptional talent, then making a commitment to excellence is simply a matter of focusing other resources.

But, what if I want to become a preeminent cancer research university? How does this organizational model differ from any discussed already in business/industry? It doesn't. You don't need to offer guaranteed lifetime employment to attract key talent to advance a discipline. Looking at the top 500 companies in the world would attest to this, as none offer guaranteed lifetime employment, yet are preeminent in their disciplines.

Without Tenure, How Do I Find a Job if Something Happens to Me?

Excellent question! There are roughly 315 million people in the United States (recognizing some are not yet working age). Given an 8 percent unemployment rate, that leaves roughly 290 million who are theoretically working. Another 1 percent of the population is tenured faculty which leaves a remaining 287 million employed people. The question is how do these people find a job if something happens to them? A full 287 million people go to work every day, contributing, adding value, advancing their organizations, and yes, worrying about their employment projections.

More education, work harder, longer hours, add value, be held accountable; these are the attributes of the working class, of which those with guaranteed lifetime employment cannot relate! Yes, those with guaranteed lifetime employment go to work most days, but not with the same concerns over their employment projections. Neither do they worry about how their organizations should change to remain competitive. For that matter, they don't even need to worry about their contribution to any change. Why, one might ask? Because tenured faculty with guaranteed lifetime employment are not impacted by change. They simply retain the status quo. The AAUP reports about 50 faculty a year lose their jobs because of university restructuring or dismissals. A fifty faculty reduction in the entire population of tenured faculty amounts to a .00002 percent unemployment rate; essentially a **zero percent** (0%) unemployment rate against a national average of eight percent (8%) as reported by the Bureau of Labor Statistics.

So, from an earlier point, with guaranteed lifetime employment, guaranteed salary, annual increases for time-in-position, and, a zero percent unemployment rate, where is the burning platform for change?

Note: Of the entire US population of more than 315 million, only 1-2 percent have doctoral degrees. That means roughly 98 percent of population do not have doctoral degrees. As well, the most recent statistics depict this group to have a 2.5 percent unemployment rate – the second lowest rate overall, and second only to those with medical or legal degrees. This directly implies that the likelihood of this group finding employment, even without tenure being available, is extremely high. In addition, when this group finds employment, their median weekly earnings are, again, second only to those with medical or legal degrees; not exactly poverty level by any means.

In the end, those with doctoral degrees are going to find a job; and this, without guaranteed lifetime employment as a hiring model.

The Academy is Not a Business!

Despite the tear-filled nostalgia that the image of college evokes – tree-shaded quads, ivy-covered, neo-Gothic buildings, and fall football weekends – the truth is that in the last two decades, higher education in the United States has evolved into a big business...there are some 5,300 colleges and universities in the US, everything from beauty schools to Harvard. They bring in $490 billion in revenue each year. They employ more than 3.5 million people. They hold more than $990 billion in assets, including cash, investments, and campuses that are essentially mini-cities. And they spend $440 billion on goods, services, and people each year (Selingo 4).

Actually, public institutions of higher education are very much a business. While their stated mission is more like that of a nonprofit than a for-profit, organizationally, they are a business. Business by definition

...is any activity that seeks profit by providing goods and services to others. Businesses provide us with food, clothing, housing, medical care, transportation, and almost everything else that makes life easier and better (Nickles 29).

Not everything that makes life easier and better is provided by businesses. Nonprofit organizations such as government agencies, public schools, associations, charities, and social causes help make the country and the world more responsive to all the needs of citizens. A nonprofit organization is an organization whose goals don't include making a personal profit for its owners. Nonprofit organizations often do strive for gains [profits]; such gains are used to meet the stated social or educational goals of the organization, not to enrich the owners... if you want to work in a nonprofit organization, you will need to learn business skills such as information management, leadership, marketing, and financial management (33).

From the highest perspective, public institutions provide a service (training and education). They provide this service to a customer (students). Public institutions receive revenue (state funding, tuition and fees, grants, development dollars...). They have expenses (personnel being the largest expense), and build and operate facility budgets; from any other perspective, they are very much a business. Public institutions of higher education, by construct, do not make profits that are returned to their shareholders, but then, neither do nonprofit organizations.

The difference is that public institutions of higher education have not had to be held accountable for efficiencies or cost growth beyond reasonable expectations from previous year expenses. This is primarily because the revenue stream came predominantly from state general fund allocations and student tuition through enrollments. Year after year, public colleges and universities simply asked for what was required to cover expenses, and generally that is what they received – this without regard to any significant cost-cutting. In those instances where the institutions did not receive sufficient funds, they raised tuition. When state general funding is decreased, then quite simply, tuition increased to help stabilize the required cost of providing the basic service of education. This cycle of loss of state general funds and increases to student tuition continues to this day. Of recent, however, is the realization that student tuition has reached unprecedented levels. This, coupled with the largest average student debt ever recorded, and the ever-rising loan-default rates, has created a tipping point like never before.

Today, the number of credible authors writing on this subject is significant. University presidents, administrators, faculty, and many other concerned taxpayers are now weighing in on the cost attendant to inefficiencies, waste, and abuse of student and taxpayer funds. It is becoming more widely recognized that public institutions of higher education are a business and should be run like one. Even non-profit organizations are run like a business; albeit they have a different mission and purpose than for-profit businesses and industries. Having sat on a board of directors for a nonprofit organization, it is easily seen that managing to a budget is required and essential to survival.

James Garland, in his book, *Saving Alma Mater* points out:

> In academia, productivity and efficiency are fighting words, and the reasons go to the heart

of the academic culture. The first reason is that efficiency and productivity are words for the business world. To professors, business represents the triumph of pragmatism over idealism. In business, employees are paid so that they will advance the interests of their employer. The primary goal of business is directed at the business itself—to increase profits and earnings, to grow sales, and to outdo the competition. By contrast, the goals of the university are not aimed at making the university better and more successful, but rather at serving the needs of society. To professors, the point of their job is to advance knowledge and transmit that knowledge to others…

Many professors dislike the clichés and catchphrases of business: "by doing more with less," "thinking outside the box," "dressing for success"…

In their view, to import the business notions of productivity and efficiency into the academy would be to push them in the direction of a lifestyle with which they are uncomfortable and for which they are ill-suited…

A second reason productivity talk raises suspicion is that it potentially threatens faculty autonomy…

If improving productivity means reducing the academic enterprise to a set of indices, benchmarks, and cost ratios, and then measuring gains by numbers on a spreadsheet, then most faculty members will want nothing to do with it...

What all of this means is that the first step toward cultural change in academia is education. No change can take place unless the university community understands fully the extent of the forces on its institution and, barring structural changes, the inevitable long-term impact of those forces (164-167).

Yet another of the biggest drivers of cost growth is unchecked program creep.

Program creep is akin to mission creep. As institutions take on more and more programs, attempting to meet more and more demands, aspirations sometimes overtake reality. With just a few more programs, two-year colleges could become four-year colleges. With just a few more graduate programs, teaching institutions could become regional or possible research institutions. The quest for more status or prestige is seen as helping improve an institution's relative position in the academic food chain...

Faculty in a department offering a baccalaureate in a particular field lust after the offering of a more prestigious and expensive, master's degree...

Growth is the operational paradigm for higher education...

Growth in enrollment means growth in revenues. Growth in revenues often leads to growth in programs. Program proliferation feeds the institution's appetite for growth in aspiration. And, institutions, overly programmed for their resources, raise prices to satiate the appetites (Dickeson 19).

Given this, we come full circle to determining which activities and initiatives should be examined and potentially modified in search of efficiencies and subsequent cost savings. All of these culprits of cost growth can be categorized into one of two general categories; low-hanging fruit and those longer-term institutional changes that are much harder to implement.

Low-hanging fruit are those things with little to no emotional impact. These are changes that, when implemented, only a very few could care enough to put forth any resistance. Any manager can make changes that are simply considered low-hanging fruit. The real challenge for any senior leader is to make the longer-term higher-impact changes that generally are structural in nature, highly emotional, and therefore subject to mass potential upheaval. The elimination of guaranteed lifetime employment (tenure) is one such structural change.

The Elimination of Tenure Would be Catastrophic to Higher Education!

It's been suggested the end of tenure would send public institutions of higher education into a tailspin, creating a loss of faculty, reduction in research dollars, donor dismay, loss of institutional status, and a whole array of unintended consequences. Everything discussed previously would say this scenario is itself grossly exaggerated and premised on unfounded fear.

While there may be a few changes in the beginning as these institutions begin to find themselves and their specific market niches, in the end, the positives will be enormous and far outweigh the potential negatives.

From above discussions, the loss of key faculty would be minimal. Those important to an institution's mission, purpose, and preeminence would be rewarded and enticed to stay, as currently exists in business and industry, in private institutions, and even in those public institutions without tenure. Most faculty with specific knowledge in a preeminent area of study will migrate to those institutions that excel in that area. For those other eighty percent of faculty (refer to Jack Welch "GE 2000 Shareholder Report" discussed above), some of which are important but not key, they will remain or not; but are interchangeable. For that bottom ten percent who would more likely leave to succeed elsewhere or in another industry altogether, the institutions would be left a better place. This also supports the bringing in of new hires; those with greater skills in technology and social media and more in tune with educational delivery methods.

Relative to research dollars, they will continue to follow the individuals who pursue them. As faculty researchers move from one institution to the next, they will continue to be active researchers, taking their knowledge and funding potential with them. This is no different than what currently happens in every personnel transaction in any institution today.

Institutions will become more focused and subsequently stronger as they move toward a system that encourages competitive challenges for personnel and resources. It may be true that through the subsequent shuffling of resources, both financial and human, some universities will gain in recognition while others may lose. This is the nature of preeminence. This is what is meant by suggesting competition is good for a free-market society and the individuals within it.

In the end, our public institutions of higher education will be stronger, more focused, considerably more efficient, and without doubt, more cost effective. Thus, overall costs to taxpayers and students will decrease, and tuition will stabilize, if not reduce.

CHAPTER 5

Alternative Solutions to Tenure

For over twenty years, highly notable authors have offered their perspectives on what should be the next evolution of guaranteed lifetime employment. While I, like others before me, push for an area ripe for change, none of us are naive enough to believe it will happen overnight; nevertheless, guaranteed lifetime employment should be eliminated. Failure to do so will certainly stymie any hope for transforming public higher education.

There are numerous alternatives put forth as replacement strategies for the current guaranteed lifetime employment practices. The following seem to recur within mainstream literature: unionization, contractual term limits, simply eliminating tenure altogether, or phasing out tenure over time.

Unionization

Unions, for all their documented ills (high wages, threat of strikes...), do provide a viable alternative to guaranteed lifetime employment. In this scenario, union contracts are negotiated, typically for a three-year period. During these negotiations, anything and everything is placed on the table. The most notable issues are generally related to pay, benefits, and job security. Having been involved in the management side of union negotiations, pay and benefits are typically financial in nature and in reality, easily negotiated to closure. (This assumes the company is financially sound, has been transparent with union membership, and is not on the precipice of requiring it go elsewhere in the world for cheaper labor.)

The hardest issue, in today's one-world concept, when negotiating a union contract stems from the threat of job loss. This happens when an organization is reacting to shareholder concerns for growth. These are much more serious negotiations and have been one of the predominant reasons for the recent reduction in union membership.

When union membership is being reduced for solid business reasons, e.g., loss of gross revenue, unions typically employ a methodology very near a last-in, first-out model. That being the last person hired will be the first person let go during difficult economic times. Ignoring technological illiteracy the cost of pay and benefits, this model seems fair enough and really does provide in some sense a comparable model to guaranteed lifetime employment. The problem, however, with employing this model in highly educated workforces, can be seen when discussing it for faculty. Technology changes so quickly as do teaching methods to accommodate today's students, that senior faculty may not be open to the effort required to adopt these many changes. Equally so, current faculty cannot be left in charge of determining structural changes to align more with business/industry either. This essentially allows the foxes to control the henhouse, very similar to current practices. Recognizing this problem, many negotiations are now slanted toward retaining those, regardless of seniority, that have the necessary skills to perform in today's ever changing and demanding workforce.

With this said, there is a renewed interest in unionizing adjunct faculty. This is in response to the mistreatment of adjuncts from tenured faculty as well as the attendant pay practices.

In a series of recent articles, there has been significant attention to the increasing numbers of adjunct hires as compared to the reduction in number of tenured faculty. "The Chronicle of Higher Education," September 15, 2014, reports from 1975 to 2011, there has been an increase of 27 percent in the number of adjunct faculty employed versus a 27 percent reduction in the number of newly tenured faculty (Schmalz 2).

In addition, a majority of the teaching positions in higher education appear to be part-time adjunct positions. And in comparing tenured versus adjunct positions, for-profits appear to be most involved in leading the adjunct hiring movement. This should come as no surprise to anyone, given for-profits do not receive state funding and therefore must run their organizations like a business. This is yet more evidence that guaranteed lifetime employment, which is not economically justifiable, has no place in for-profit organizations which must run efficiently and effectively, or perish.

Given then, the growing number of adjunct faculty (Brauer 2), the significant pay gap between tenured professors and adjuncts, the continual mistreatment of adjuncts by tenured faculty, and the growing resentment of adjuncts to these perceived injustices, it's apparent why unions have become an increasingly attractive alternative (Jerde 3).

In an article titled "Power in Numbers" published in *The Chronicle of Higher Education*, April 14, 2014, the author quotes one of the many adjuncts interviewed as saying "...there is sort of an accumulation of indignities that one experiences when you are teaching here...I think we will continue to get exploited, and things will get worse and worse, if we don't do something" (1).

This and similar mindsets and experiences has prompted union organizations to gain interest and membership across major metropolitan areas including Boston, Connecticut, Los Angeles, Maryland, Minneapolis/St. Paul, New York State, Philadelphia, Pittsburgh, San Francisco, Seattle/Tacoma, St. Louis and Washington (Brauer 28).

Contract Term-Limits

Perhaps a better approach and certainly one most suggested, is providing term limits versus tenure. This model is being employed today in some of the more innovative and cutting edge institutions of higher education.

Lawrence S. Bacow, former chancellor of the Massachusetts Institute of Technology (and former president of Tufts), has suggested that:

> ...universities might consider limiting tenure to some number of years. The objective would be to combat the costly and sometimes corrosive effects of the end to mandatory retirement. I should confess that when I was a beginning graduate student I was one of those who objected to mandatory retirement, which was legal at the time. I was in the last class that the brilliant economist Jacob Viner ever taught at Princeton on the history of economic though. Summoning up all my courage, I went into Professor Viner's office to complain about his impending retirement. Viner gave me one of his most piercing looks and said, with a twinkle in his eye: "Mr. Bowen, most of what you say is true. I am at the peak of my powers, smarter than all of my colleagues, and it would be a shame if future Princeton students were deprived of the opportunity to learn from me. But," he added, "your conclusion is wrong. I should be forced to retire. I'll tell you why. My colleagues are good and compassionate people, and they will never distinguish me from

all of the other faculty members who should have retired years ago! Either all of us go, or none of us goes. It is much better that all of us go." Here is the end of the story: Professor Viner did have to retire from Princeton, but he went on to each at leading universities all over the world until his death (Bowen 14).

Term limits, alternatively called renewable long-term contracts, have been discussed by many. The Center for College Affordability and Productivity (CCAP) states:

> ...this alternative involves the elimination of tenure in favor of long-term renewable contracts for faculty. The contracts could be structured for an initial probationary period of three to five years, with the criteria for performance evaluation (a detailed outline of teaching, scholarly, and service expectations) specified in the contract, including a clause pertaining to academic freedom to avoid its diminishment. If after the probationary period, a faculty member passed his/her performance review and there was still a need for the position at the college, then the contract would be renewed, with a subsequent performance review similar to the initial one. This contract renewal process would continue, with perhaps an increase in the length of additional contracts, not to exceed ten years, as a reward for continued successful performance (21).

ALTERNATIVE SOLUTIONS TO TENURE

Renewable term-limit contracts address the problematic issues of tenure without eliminating the clause for academic freedom. These types of contracts would provide colleges and universities the freedom to move faculty as required to maintain a competitive position in the global economy. The CCAP elaborates on this type of legally binding agreement by saying:

> The contracts would give colleges more flexibility when it comes to adjusting staff levels in response to changes in consumer demand or the economy, as well as the ability to rid themselves of faculty that have become deadwood in a reasonable timeframe, as opposed to being stuck with unproductive faculty members until retirement or death. The specification of performance evaluation criteria in employment contracts would help clarify the reward structure for individual faculty. This sort of contractual arrangement would be more cost effective for colleges than the tenure system, as it would free up long-term resource obligations in favor of shorter-term obligations with comparable compensation packages.
>
> ...The Franklin W. Olin College is a private undergraduate engineering school in Massachusetts that opened its doors for its first class in 2002. Rather than offering tenure, Olin hires faculty with a system of five-year renewable contracts. When negotiating terms, faculty

members and the college agree on the criteria that will be used in a peer reviewed performance evaluation when the contract is up for renewal. Despite not offering tenure, the college was able to attract what it describes as a "dream team" staff by luring both tenured and tenure-track faculty from prestigious institutions such as MIT, Cornell, and Vanderbilt.

One might suspect that Olin necessarily offer faculty a risk premium as a tradeoff for the absence of tenure, but this assertion is not supported by the faculty compensation data... average salary, benefits and total compensation package of all professors at fifteen of the top engineering colleges in the US in 2007 [reflected below] depicts Olin professors received the 7th highest total compensation among the schools, but earned the 6th highest average salary. Olin's faculty compensation package is competitive without a tenure policy, suggesting that the model of long-term renewable contracts has bona fide merit in the real world.

The potential downfall of these proposed term-limits arises if the renewal is the sole determination of a voting board made up entirely of tenured faculty. If this happens, then nothing has changed. The current system in place simply manifests itself under the guise of term-limit renewal versus promotion and tenure deliberation.

Simply Phasing It Out

Most would probably agree there will not be cliffhanger scenarios, meaning tenure will not simply cease to exist. Nothing as embedded in our society as tenure can simply exist one day and not exist the next. There are entire industries built in support of tenure, for example, the whole publish or perish paper and journal submission enterprise. Conferences survive and in fact thrive only because assistant and associate faculty have to publish in order to gain the next hierarchical level on the tenure track: assistants to associates and associates to full professors. Doing a simple Google search produces hundreds upon hundreds of scholarly conferences, if not thousands depending on how you count them. These industries, not to mention certification institutions and similarly situated organizations, exist predominantly for advancing the surgically intertwined tenure process. Could these entities exist beyond tenure? Absolutely! These and other organizations certainly can survive if for no other reason than they provide a medium for exchange of information. Generally, most of these types of organizations have aligned themselves to specific disciplines. In doing so, they have created a membership of similarly minded or interested individuals. This in itself will help ensure the continuation of these similarly situated organizations and conferences.

So, given related and attendant industries can survive without tenure, then let's turn our attention to the phasing out of guaranteed lifetime employment (tenure). Phasing out tenure is not unlike the many other things that business and industry phase out. As public institutions of higher education, we simply draw a line in the sand saying that tenure will not be granted going forward. Those who currently have tenure will continue to have tenure and those who do not will be issued some other form, as described above, of employment contract (perhaps, contract term limits, etc.). For those who have tenure, there will also be an age cap at which their tenure ceases to exist; for example, their full social security age. *While this seems to run counter to the elimination of forced age retirement laws, it really is quite different. A college or university is not saying they are firing the tenured individual, they are simply saying their guaranteed right to employment no longer exists and they become like others after them who were not granted tenure.*

Mediating to a Successful Resolution

The differences reflected in the previous discussion between the interests of the tenured faculty and those of the university and student can be resolved. The process for resolving these differences in concern is through an oft-used process called mediation.

Mediation is a process for resolving disputes, where an intermediary helps conflicting parties engage in conversation to jointly resolve their concerns.

As a process, mediation follows an organic sequence that unfolds differently in each situation, but still has recognizable phases. Usually parties have specific disputes, incidents, disagreements, and concerns that have brought them to mediation, things they want changed. The mediation may also address underlying conflicts and systemic causes, if the parties want to take on that larger project.

The intermediary is literally "one who goes between." By definition, a mediator has some degree of impartiality and detachment from the outcome. Mediators guide the process; however, *the parties* do the work of corning up with the solutions and making the decisions. The parties may be a person, a group, or a whole nation who come as a unit to the mediation, or are represented there, and who share a common identity or interest. One way out of conflict is through dialogue – talking and listening directly to each other. Dialogue broadens the parties' understanding of their situation, of each other, and of their desired future. This is rarely a neat or rational process! The goal of mediation is to determine workable, durable solutions that meet the participants' practical, emotional, and social concerns as fully as possible. Mediators work to create a cooperative atmosphere for problem solving where the parties themselves plan how they wish to proceed, individually and collectively.

What makes mediation effective as a problem-resolution tool is that it begins and ends with the deepest concerns (interests, not positions) of each party. Mediation takes seriously those concerns that each party says matters the most to them, whether it is fairness, justice, recognition, respect, inclusivity or simply a topic which is highly emotionally charged. Through the mediation process, each party gets a chance to express their concerns and emotions.

Each party is allowed to openly and freely discuss whatever concerns them, which sometimes takes another path from the topic at hand.

The mediation process provides a basic structure for problem resolution. It provides a forum for private and caring conversations where each party gets to speak openly, without fear of retribution. This, in itself, provides the opportunity for trust building and venting such that parties may move more readily to the healing phase of the basic model of hurt and loss.

If one of the parties is fixated on continuing the conflict or "winning" the negotiation, then mediation, or any other process for that matter, is not going to work. Mediation works best when both parties DO want to end the conflict and find a meaningful resolution that allows a continuation of a normal life process.

The basic mediation process (Beer & Packard 7) contains similar elements regardless of the topic or concern of the parties. And, if we think about the process described below, it really is the same process we use in our family and personal lives.

The mediation process begins with people from each party voicing their concerns and listing their issues. This step is generally highly charged and emotionally laden. As much as one would like to be able to express rational, methodical thoughts, this first step does not normally take this form.

The second step, however, is where each party begins the process of more clearly identifying their real concerns, anxieties, and fears. It is in this second step that each party may be considerably more capable of voicing their deepest fears.

The third step of the process is where real progress is made. This step involves problem solving. This is where each party begins to nudge towards the other's position. Mediation is a negotiation of some sorts. In the end, no one party gets everything they want, and in fact, no one party may be happy in their entirety with the outcome. The point of mediation and negotiation as a whole is to move towards something both parties can deal with – perhaps financially, or perhaps simply emotionally.

The fourth and final step is to document what has been agreed to. It is during this phase that the real nitty-gritty details are fleshed out and documented.

In the final analysis, the whole process is uniquely molded to fit the parties of the mediation. What each party brings to the table in terms of past experiences, emotions, mental models, and all other forms of historical context, form the mediation process and outcomes.

If we were to pretend we were using a mediation process to resolve the issue of guaranteed lifetime employment in public institutions of higher education, the following scenario is perhaps what step-one might look like:

Step #1

Tenured faculty: "We want to be part of the governance of the university. The university would not exist if not for us, the tenured faculty. We are the university. In the beginning, it was one professor and one student meeting in a pub, for example, where the intellectual exchange of ideas and freedom to think abstractly took place. The university was formed from this very personal one-on-one relationship. It wasn't until the number of students became greater that administration was asked to join the University of Scholars. Universities are about learning and research; they are about serving the greater good."

Universities/Colleges: "We understand the importance of tenured faculty needing to be part of the institutional administration. We understand tenured faculty need the freedom to teach and convey the importance of subject matter in a manner that will most leave an impression. We understand the need for freedom to create courses, curriculum, and support material for the purposes of transferring and perpetuating knowledge. But in the end, we have a business to run. We need to be able to make changes as appropriate; to merge discipline areas (departments, colleges, schools) within the greater university structure. We need to be able to cut costs by reducing programs and areas that do not have a positive return on investment. We need to bring in newer, more technologically astute faculty. We need to be able to serve the taxpayers, students, and nation by running the university like a business versus a passive, taxpayer supported and tuition-raising institution."

Step #2

Tenured faculty: Our real concerns can be narrowed to the following:

- We want job security
- We want to own our curriculum and courses
- We want the freedom to teach without fear of retribution from the administration of the university

Colleges/Universities: Our goals are:

- Freedom to run the university in an efficient manner
- Freedom to make changes that impact costs
- Freedom to merge or restructure units
- Freedom to eliminate programs, curriculums and courses with a negative return on investment

From this point, a meaningful conversation can evolve. Clearly from the above, guaranteed lifetime employment has meaning to tenured faculty as their number one concern and desire. This thread runs counter to the interests of the public institution. Most other items on either list can be readily dealt with, but guaranteed lifetime employment, in our scenario above, requires resolution.

CHAPTER 6

Conclusion

There Are No Problems in Academia That Have Not Already Been Solved

No problems exist in academia that have not already been solved in business and industry, some as many as 25 years ago. Reducing academic units through merging of similar academic threads, centralizing common functions, and eliminating academic programs that fail to offer a reasonable return on investment-are all examples of applying successful business principals to academia. Along with these, eliminating guaranteed lifetime employment will provide impetus toward stabilizing and ultimately reducing student tuition rates and better utilizing taxpayer dollars. Similar experiences in business and industry have already proven the increases in efficiency and cost reduction.

After serving for nearly thirty years with a major "Fortune 100" defense contractor, and having been a member of the transition management teams through multiple major mergers/acquisitions, I have been trained to identify inefficiencies and take corrective measures. *The reported problems in academia have all been previously addressed and solved; they are not new; they are however, woefully unaddressed and more pronounced.*

There have been a multitude of books, articles, and white papers written describing the problems with rising tuition, student debt, and their long-term impact on our economy. Total student debt has already surpassed 1.3 trillion dollars. Since 1970, the annual costs for four-year colleges have risen three times faster than the rate of inflation (Selingo xiv).

Graduates leave college with an average of $29,400 in student loans only to find a tight job market and poor economic conditions. Consequently, a greater number of students are moving back home, postponing marriage and family, and are crippled in their ability to purchase the cars, homes, and furnishings typical of previous generations. Numerous literary works blame the rising cost of education on the ever-increasing building of physical facilities or the proliferation of administration. While physical facilities certainly play a role in rising tuition, there seems to be little argument for administration being a significant cost driver; rather, increases in administration have trailed increasing enrollments, or have been used as a multiplier to increasing overall enrollments.

CONCLUSION

The elephant in the room, one addressed time and again by business and industry, are the inefficiencies and cost implications of guaranteed lifetime employment, more generally known as tenure in academia. Tenure promotes inefficiency and subsequently increases costs.

Taxpayer funding (free money), year-over-year salary increases for time-in-position and guaranteed lifetime employment create artificial expectations of entitlement, discourages the 'burning platform effect' any sense of urgency, and encourages complacency and inefficiency. In other words, as a faculty member, "...why do I need to do anything other than what I wish to do? My salary will always be there, I will always get an increase just for continuing my service, and you can't fire me unless I commit an illegal act."

Most organizations cannot protect a cost-driver that doesn't have an economic right to exist; for-profit and not-for-profit organizations in business and industry have been managed by this tenant for years.

The remnants of guaranteed lifetime employment in areas other than academia were dismantled in the U.S. many years ago. This antiquated policy, characterized by the tenure system, fails to create the much-needed sense of urgency, which forms the underlying premise of efficiency gains. Without this underlying premise, higher education institutions experience increased costs and subsequently higher tuition rates.

The current tenure practice has another dark side which has been documented many times – namely discriminatory practices. The tenure selection process generally lacks objective and measurable criteria to determine tenure applicability. The subjective determination of tenure is premised on whether the individual being evaluated is generally liked. This is set forth by blind (secretly cast) vote of the tenure committee. This behavior is condoned and deemed appropriate through the concept of *"collegiality"*; i.e., "...we do not like you because you do not fit in." Without objective and measurable criteria, fewer females and underrepresented minorities are provided equitable opportunities. The fact of this is easily founded in the underrepresentation of female and minority faculty across our colleges and universities. It is also seen in the annual requirement for faculty search committees to attend basic training for diversity awareness in hiring.

Concerns over academic freedom are cited as reasoning for tenure; however, recent nationwide faculty survey data dispels that myth. Rather, surveys suggest the number one reason listed by tenured faculty for continuing tenure practices is not having to worry about future employment perils associated with economically driven enterprises (Naomi 130). As unionization was created at the onset of America's industrialization period to counter unfair labor practices, so too was tenure created to protect once-needed academic freedom.

Tenure is a relic of past times. In today's global economic environment, tenure struggles to defend its place in public higher education. Hiring the best personnel – those who are technologically competent and can offer tools for today's college student – is hindered by a lack of financial resources. Yet, the necessary financial resources are available (Dickeson 1), only they are allocated to those who cannot be removed because of their "right" to guaranteed lifetime employment. Perhaps worst of all, the resources might be allocated to those who are the least likely to provide the technology and tools demanded of today's knowledge economy. *This is a skills mix issue that is not allowed to be solved in academia; but is readily solved in business and industry.*

Organizational models represent the way work gets done. Centralized models provide for the care of those in a given function or discipline by ensuring that common practices, policies, and methodologies are followed across all departments or tiered organizations. Aside from creating a more highly advanced knowledge model, centralization supports the movement of people as business needs change. Decentralization, on the other hand, provides the freedom for the organizational entity (department or tiered organization) to hire who they wish for what purpose they deem appropriate. In this model, people performing the same function may not have the same entry qualifications or even possess the same general knowledge as peers in other organizational entities.

Decentralization also creates an "ownership" of the people in the decentralized organization. In general, decentralization creates variable knowledge and increases resources which in turn increase costs. Hence, as senior leaders seek efficiencies, they frequently turn to centralized forms of organizational models.

Reorganizing for efficiency in public institutions of higher education is severely hampered by the misinterpretation of the concept of shared governance and requirements to gain approval of tenured faculty before curriculum or course modifications.

The problem is not a lack of taxpayer funding, but a more efficient use of said funds. Lifetime employment (tenure) is a major contributing factor to the rise of student tuition and many other ills, as described above. Decentralization as well plays a major role in inefficiencies and increased costs, albeit second to the tenure process.

I recently presented a paper at a conference in Chicago, Illinois. While attending an evening social, I was standing in line at the cash bar awaiting my soft drink. The woman behind me struck up a conversation. The conversation, which started very casually, became one of the most open and honest conversations I have ever participated in with another academic. This individual was a senior executive at a very prestigious, fully online university.

Our conversation started with a general discussion on how online education was disrupting the traditional model of brick and mortar universities. We quickly did a deeper dive into how predictive analytics and self-grading software were the next great move in this very immature online marketplace, and, how these predictive analytic tools would very quickly make obsolete even the current online university models. As it turned out, this individual was preparing a presentation to prominent officials on this very topic. Her ideas and mine

CONCLUSION

were fully synchronized to the point that she evolved her presentation in real-time as we spoke.

This conversation quickly led to the next topic of tenure in academia. She made the unsolicited comment that she had been a full, tenured professor, and had resigned to pursue positions where she could make a greater impact on future generations. To this end, she took her current position as a university executive administrator at a private university. She indicated that, as a fully tenured professor, she did not like the pettiness, immaturity, and self-centeredness the tenure path afforded. She felt her ability to create change among her colleagues was non-existent.

I queried her on how her current university dealt with tenure. She replied they did not have tenure. Instead, her university offered salaries very competitive to business and industry, and – this is where it gets really exciting – they offer end of the year results sharing based on profit forecasts and actual returns! I noted that it was a standard argument; if a university did not offer guaranteed lifetime employment, then that university would not be able to attract the best and brightest. To this she shrugged saying this just simply wasn't so. She added they have some of the best and brightest on staff, and for every position that comes available they have hundreds who apply. She correctly made reference to the fact that there were thousands of highly qualified professionals and a great many of those with earned doctorates who just want to do what they have been schooled to do: teach. She said it was a façade that a university could not hire the best and brightest if they did not offer tenure; that her university and Olin college were examples of models that run counter to this faculty – propagated myth.

I commented to her that we were a public institution of higher education and as such, state funding had recently been dwindling. Her comment was to paraphrase Clayton Christensen in his book *The Innovative University* saying: of all the existing old school brick and mortar models of higher education, disruptive educational models would reduce these by fifty percent at some point in the future. She acknowledged the more preeminent ones would most likely survive, although it would not be obvious what they might look like in the future. Her comment that followed could not have mapped better to this text if I had wanted it to; she said the single greatest threat to the transformation of public higher education was tenure! Her description of the evils of entitlement stemming from tenure could not have been more right on. She described the "I don't have to do anything I don't want to do and you can't fire me" syndrome. Having been a full, tenured professor appeared to heighten her awareness of this reality. We talked at great length on our common observations. She noted those with tenure have no reason to promote change; that their employment was guaranteed for life unless something radical happened, like the elimination of specific programs, which she accurately commented does not happen often enough to ever raise alarm.

Her next comments resonated with my own experiences in business and industry. She said all of us were businesses and should be run like one! I said these types of comments in my alma mater were like asking for a fight. I told her how many times I made reference to accountability, return on investment and other such things to those in academia, and how others nearly threw me out of their offices on hearing this. To those I spoke with, saying we were a business, albeit not a very well run one, were fighting words. She laughed and said it was not uncommon, as she too had heard this many times. She then stated, if the free taxpayer money ever really does dry-up, those who do not acknowledge public institutions of higher education as businesses will see differently, because the required change will be more than simply finding cost savings through the low-hanging fruit.

In 2005, a bipartisan congressional group asked the National Academies to identify the key steps which Congress should take to ensure a science and technology enterprise which would enable the U.S. to compete in the global economy of the 21st century. In response, the National Academies appointed a committee that produced *Rising Above the Gathering Storm: Energizing and Employing America for a Brighter Economic Future.*

That report provided a powerful framework for discussing America's competitiveness as well as recommendations that formed the basis of the America COMPETES Act. Four years later, in 2009, Senators Lamar Alexander and Barbara Mikulski and Representatives Bart Gordon and Ralph Hall requested that the National Academies provide a follow-up report that examines more deeply the health and competitiveness of the nation's research universities (NRC 2).

The committee was charged with the following task:

> An ad hoc committee will author a consensus report with findings and recommendations that answer the question:
>
> What are the top ten actions that Congress, the Federal Government, state governments, research universities, and others could take to assure the ability of the American research university to maintain the excellence in research and doctoral education needed to help the United States compete, prosper, and achieve national goals for health, energy, the environment, and security in the global community of the 21st century? (x).

Of the ten recommendations from the committee, recommendation number four read:

Recommendation 4

> Increase university cost-effectiveness and productivity in order to provide a greater return on investment for taxpayers, philanthropists, corporations, foundations, and other research sponsors.
>
> **Actors and Actions — Implementing Recommendation 4:**

CONCLUSION

Universities: The nation's research universities should set and achieve bold goals in cost-containment, efficiency, and productivity in business operations and academic programs. Universities should strive to constrain the cost escalation of all ongoing activities – academic and auxiliary – to the inflation rate or lower through improved efficiency and productivity. Beyond the implementation of efficient business practices, universities should review existing academic programs from the perspectives of centrality, quality, and cost-effectiveness, adopting modern instructional methods such as cyber learning, and encouraging greater collaboration among research investigators and institutions, particularly in the acquisition and utilization of expensive research equipment and facilities.

Expected Outcomes

...by increasing cost-effectiveness and productivity, institutions will realize significant cost savings in their operations that may be used to improve performance by shifting resources strategically and/or to reduce growth in their need for resources (e.g., tuition).... (13).

In a recent article (Coy, 2013), Eric Schmidt, Google Executive Chairman and Anne-Marie Slaughter, former Department of State official, were quoted as saying "...*colleges have the luxury of thorough democratic deliberation of issues because they never actually do anything...traditional colleges and universities, with their high fixed costs, are at risk*" (1).

To this end, eliminating guaranteed lifetime employment will increase cost-effectiveness and productivity, providing impetus toward stabilizing and ultimately reducing current student tuition rates.

To better understand the seriousness of the tenure issue and the numerous attendant implications of it, this work focused on not only the problems with tenure, but to be worth anything at all, the alternative solutions to the antiquated tenure debacle.

Guaranteed Lifetime Employment Runs Counter to Three Basic Tenants of Efficiency and Cost Containment

Guaranteed lifetime employment runs counter to three basic tenants of efficiency and cost containment: (1) it creates an unjustifiable and unsustainable long-term financial commitment on the part of the college/university (45+ years), (2) it creates a sense of entitlement, which, premised on fear, runs counter to creating efficiencies and reducing costs, and (3) as a process, it is biased, prejudicial and widely recognized as inherently discriminatory.

Guaranteed lifetime employment is proven to be discriminatory. Classes and workshops around the nation are beginning

CONCLUSION

to heighten our awareness of this issue; a topic of concern which is long overdue for discussion. In short:

- The guaranteed lifetime employment (tenure) process is a closed system promoting bias and perpetuation of sameness which directly, inherently, statistically, and visually contributes to discriminatory practices.
- The guaranteed lifetime employment (tenure) process uses groupthink and coercion to accomplish its purpose.
- With an unemployment rate of nearly 8 percent, where highly educated men and women cannot find gainful employment, but yet are qualified to teach difficult and complex subjects; guaranteed lifetime employment seems indefensible.
- Where there is a proliferation of highly qualified and intelligent PhDs who cannot teach because of those who continue to occupy tenured positions well past normal retirement age, sucking up valuable college and university, taxpayer dollars, guaranteed lifetime employment seems irrational and perhaps even subversive to higher education's true mission.

Guaranteed lifetime employment is not necessary. This given:

- *The Chronicle of Higher Education* conducted research of 1,251 U.S. colleges, and found that public institutions pay professors very competitive salaries, while also boasting the lowest ratio of students to faculty members, than colleges in any other country

globally [public institutions also paid highly competitive rates in comparison to business/industry] (10).
- Tenured faculty pay is not an argument for offering guaranteed lifetime employment.
- Public institutions of higher education can attract the best and brightest without the guarantee of lifetime employment, as has been done by other universities/colleges (Olin College as an example) as well as business and industry.
- We can keep people from leaving our public institutions of higher education, without the guarantee of lifetime employment, through better utilization of a proven career development model and other successful retention strategies.
- Academic freedom is no longer an issue with the First Amendment to the United States Constitution and the court systems.

Guaranteed lifetime employment runs counter to nearly every attempt to make infrastructure changes that can transform public institutions of higher education.

Public institutions of higher education are a business. While their mission statements might be more closely aligned to nonprofit than for-profit organizations, they are nonetheless a business; albeit not a very efficient one.

Taxpayer funding (free money), year-after-year salary increases for time-in-position, and guaranteed lifetime employment create artificial expectations of entitlement, discourage

CONCLUSION

the burning platform effect (sense of urgency), and encourage complacency and inefficiency.

Guaranteed lifetime employment promotes a skills mix issue that is not allowed to be solved in public institutions of higher education, but is readily solved in business and industry.

With guaranteed lifetime employment, guaranteed salary, annual increases for time-in-position, and a zero percent unemployment rate, where is the burning platform for change?

The cost to maintain guaranteed lifetime employment practices, where a faculty member is assured salary, time-in-position increases, full benefits and a handsome retirement match is an unsustainable cost the institution must endure for 40 plus years with each tenured position.

We have numerous disruptors to our current public higher educational model which are changing the landscape of public higher education, creating skill discrepancies with existing, less technology-oriented faculty:

- On-line learning and resources.
- Massive Open On-line Courses (MOOCs); being offered for free by some of the most prestigious universities in the world.
- The for-profit sector of higher education is providing quality education at a much lower and highly profitable price, without the offer of guaranteed lifetime employment.

- Accountability and public scrutiny are increasing at a significantly greater pace than ever before; taxpayer upheaval is taking root.
- There exists a significant and well documented dissatisfaction with current graduating students; this is a direct reflection of our institutions' unsatisfactory objectives and teaching/learning methodologies.
- Education is becoming considerably less place bound, diminishing the perceived need for brick and mortar institutions.
- Many new, effective learning models are evolving that go beyond class lecture only, to the application of assimilated knowledge through evidenced skills.

Although it may sound like an emotional position, guaranteed lifetime employment is simply not fair or economically defensible.

In the throes of our many U.S. recessions, the most recent being December 2007 through June 2009, thousands of hard working men and women, many highly skilled, lost their jobs. The public perceptions of guaranteed lifetime employment cannot help but question its fairness.

In the light of the worst housing crises ever experienced in the history of the United States, where many non-deserving human beings, brothers and sisters of our national populace, lost their only form of shelter, sending many to the ranks of poverty; guaranteed lifetime employment seems unfair.

CONCLUSION

Providing guaranteed lifetime employment, in the eyes of the public, at a time when unemployment is hovering around eight percent and people change jobs anywhere from eight to twelve times in their careers, just doesn't seem fair.

When everyone else is struggling to make ends meet, living through recessions as best they can, guaranteeing someone lifetime employment, again, just doesn't seem fair.

When families want their children to go to college to idealistically have better lives than their own, yet the cost of college makes educating our youth unattainable, guaranteeing someone lifetime employment just doesn't seem fair.

To repeat, no country or business outside of public higher education provides this level of security. Tenure, guaranteed lifetime employment, simply runs against those who produce more, are accountable, and have to compete in a continually evolving global economy. The public is beginning to move from apathy to resentment of what appears an undeserving and economically infeasible and indefensible benefit.

We all recognize life isn't fair. If you don't like something, then don't just sit and whine about it, do something, as the saying goes. That's what this book is intended to do... something. That something is to heighten awareness to the single greatest threat to the transformation of public institutions of higher education – guaranteed lifetime employment.

A literature review suggests the elimination of guaranteed lifetime employment in public institutions of higher education has been a topic of debate for over twenty-five years. Until recently, it appears to have fallen on deaf ears. Times are changing however, and recent information, which on the surface appears to be nothing more than disjointed data points, is coming together to form a solid and obvious argument for its elimination.

Given all of the above, it is not obvious what justification exists for the continuance of the practice of awarding guaranteed lifetime employment. When all of this is placed together, we see an antiquated educational model that surely will experience a major change as time goes forward. In looking at guaranteed lifetime employment, the most costly remnant of a time gone by, it can be seen how this too, has run its course and is, for all of the reasons cited above, time to be retired.

Bibliography

AACS. (2019). *Community College Enrollment Crisis? Historical Trends in Community College Enrollment.* American Association of Community Colleges. September 7, 2019.

AARP. (2020). *The Longevity Economy Outlook. How People Age 50 and Older are Fueling Economic Growth, Stimulating Jobs, and Creating Opportunities for All.* Downloaded from https://www.aarp.org/content/dam/aarp/research/surveys_statistics/econ/2019/longevity-economy-outlook.doi.10.26419-2Fint.00042.001.pdf.

Abrams, D. (2011). *Man down: Proof beyond a reasonable doubt that women are better cops, drivers, gamblers, spies, world leaders, beer tasters, hedge fund managers, and just about everything else.* New York: Abrams.

Ackerman, S. (2011, July 26). Navy's next laser mashes up machine guns and death rays. *Wired Online.* http://www.wired.com/dangerroom/2011/07/navys-next-laser-mashes-up-machine-guns-and-death-rays.

Allen, E., Hubain, B., Hunt, C., Lucero, S., & Stewart, S. (2019). Race Matters: Implementing Racial Identity Development Theories into the Classroom. 2012 Diversity Summit. May 4, 2012, downloaded from https://www.racialequitytools.org/resourcefiles/Race%20 Matters_%20Implementing%20Racial%20Identity%20 Development%20Theories%20into%20the%20 Classroom.pdf.

Alsop, R. (2008). *The trophy kids grow up: How the Millennial Generation is shaking up the workplace.* San Francisco: Jossey-Bass.

Anderson, D. R., Sweeney, D. J., Williams, T. A., Camm, J. D., & Martin, R. K. (2011). *An introduction to management science: Quantitative approaches to decision making* (13th ed.). Mason, OH: South Western Cengage Learning.

Allen, I., & Seaman, J (2017). Digital Learning Compass: Distance Education Enrollment Report 2017. Babson Survey Research Group.

Annis, B. & Gray, J. (2013). *Work with Me: The 8 Blind Spots Between Men and Women in Business.* New York, N.Y.: Palgrave McMillan.

Annis, B. and Merron, K. 2014. Gender Intelligence: Breakthrough Strategies for Increasing Diversity and Improving Your Bottom Line. New York, N.Y.: Palgrave McMillan.

Annis, B. & Nesbitt, R. (2017). Results at the Top: Using Gender Intelligence to Create Breakthrough Growth. Hoboken, N.J., John Wiley & Sons, Inc.

American Psychological Association (APA), (2018). Stress in America: Generation Z. Stress in America Survey.

Arias, E. (2006). *United States life tables, 2003.* National Vital Statistics Reports (Center for Disease Control and Prevention), 54(14).

Arnold, C. (2019). *Student Loans A Lot Like the Subprime Mortgage Debacle, Watchdog Says*. NPR. December 9, 2019, downloaded from https://www.npr.org/2019/12/09/785527874/student-loans-a-lot-like-the-subprime-mortgage-debacle-watchdog-says.

Banaji, M. & Greenwald, A. (2016). Blind Spot: Hidden Biases of Good People. New York, N.Y., Bantam.

Bardwick, J. (1991). *Danger in the comfort zone*. New York: AMACOM.

Bargh, J. (2017). *Before You Know It*. New York, N.Y., Simon & Schuster.

Barker, J. (2006, October 10). Wealth, innovation and diversity video. Retrieved from http://www.mediapartners.com/leadership/wealth_innovation_and_diversity.htm

Bauer-Wolf, J. (2020). *7 Higher Education Trends to Watch in 2020*. Education Drive. January 1, 2020, downloaded from https://www.educationdive.com/news/7-higher-education-trends-to-watch-in-2020/569629/.

Begley, S. (2007, July 2). When Does Your Brain Stop Making New Neurons? *Newsweek*, 62–64.

Berger, K. S., & Thompson, R. A. (1998). *The developing person through the life span* (4th ed.). New York: Worth.

Berk, L. E. (2009). *Development through the lifespan* (5th ed.). Boston: Pearson Education.

Bertoline, G. (2011, March 23). *Future college of technology: A vision-based detailed analysis and implementation plan*. Presented at the Purdue University College of Technology Dean Search Seminar. http://www.tech.purdue.edu/About_Us/Office-of-the-Dean/documents/Bertoline-presentation.pdf.

Black. (2022). Explanation and Types of Doctorates. *Black Ph.D. / Ed.D. Magazine Online.* Downloaded from the internet December 20, 2021. http://blackphdeddmagazine.com/Explanation_and_Types_of_Doctorates.html.

Blanchard, B. S., & Fabrycky, W. J. (2011). *Systems engineering and analysis* (5th ed.). Upper Saddle River, NJ: Prentice Hall.

BLS (Bureau of Labor Statistics). (2015). Monthly Labor Review. December, 2015, downloaded from https://www.bls.gov/opub/mlr/2015/article/overview-of-projections-to-2024.htm.

Blumenstyk, G. (2018). *The Adult Student.* The Chronicle of Higher Education.

Blumenstyk, G. (2019). *The Innovation Imperative: The Buzz, The Barriers, and What Real Change Looks Like.* The Chronicle of Higher Education.

Bodnar, A. G., Ouellette, M., Frolkis, M., Holt, S. E., Chiu, C. P., Morin, G. B., . . . Harley, C. B. (1998, January 16). Extension of lifespan by introduction of telomerase into normal human cells. *Science, 279,* 349–352.

Boeckenstedt, J. (2019). *Where Did All the Students Go?* The Chronicle Review. October 2, 2019.

Boone, E. J., Safrit, R. D., & Jones, J. (2002). *Developing programs in adult education: A conceptual programming model* (2nd ed.). Long Grove, IL: Waveland.

Boroush, M. (2010). *NSF releases new statistics on business innovation* (NSF 11-300). Washington, D.C.: National Science Foundation.

Boston Consulting Group. (2011). Global Tanet Risk – Seven Responses.

Boston Consulting Group. (2024). Who's Winning the Global Race for STEM and AI Talent?.

Boyd, D., & Bee, H. L. (2011). *Lifespan development* (6th ed.). New York: Pearson Education.

Bransberger, P., & Michealu, D. (2016). *Knocking at the College Door – Projections of High School Graduates.* Western Interstate Commission for Higher Education, Updated July 2017.

Bridges, W. (2009). *Managing transitions: Making the most of change.* Philadelphia, PA: Perseus Books Group.

Bronson, P., & Merryman, A. (2013). *Top dog.* New York: Twelve, Hachette Book Company.

Brown, E. (2007, August 13). A Path out of the forest. *Forbes,* 92–94.

Bucher, R. (2000). *Diversity Consciousness.* Upper Saddle River, NJ.; Prentice Hall.

Bureau of Labor Statistics. (2016). *Occupational Outlook Handbook.* Washington, DC: US Department of Labor. http://www.bls.gov/ooh/.

Business-Higher Education Forum (BHEF). (2005). *A commitment to America's future: Responding to the crisis in mathematics and science education.* Washington, D.C.: Business-Higher Education Forum.

Busta, H. (2019). *Higher Ed Enrollment Reaches 10 Year Low, Federal Data Shows.* Education Drive. December 16, 2019, downloaded from https://www.educationdive.com/news/higher-ed-enrollment-reaches-10-year-low-federal-data-shows/569091/.

Carlson, S. (2018). *Sustaining the College Business Model.* The Chronicle of Higher Education.

Carlson, S. (2020). *The Oddsmakers of the College Deathwatch.* The Chronicle of Higher Education.

Cateora, P. R. (1990). *International marketing* (7th ed.). Homewood, IL: Irwin.

CCAP. (2010). *25 Ways to Reduce the Cost of College.* A Policy Paper from the Center for Affordability and Productivity. September 2010. Downloaded from the internet December 5, 2017. http://www.centerforcollegeaffordability.org/uploads/25Ways_to_Reduce_the_Cost_of_College.pdf.

Cellini, S. (2018). Gainfully Employed? New Evidence on the Earnings, Employment and Debt of For-Profit Certificate Students. Brookings Institute. Retrieved from https://www.brookings.edu/blog/brown-center-chalkboard/2018/02/09/gainfully-employed-new-evidence-on-the-earnings-employment-and-debt-of-for-profit-certificate-students/

Centro Nacional de Investigaciones Oncologicas (CNIO). (2012, May 14). First gene therapy successful against aging associated decline: Mouse lifespan extended up to 24% with a single treatment. *Science Daily.* http://www.sciencedaily.com/releases/2012/05/120514204050.htm

CHE. (2019). *New Financial Models in Higher Education.* The Chronicle of Higher Education. July 8, 2019.

Cherniss, C., & Adler, M. (2000). *Promoting emotional intelligence in organizations.* Alexandria, VA.: American Society for Training and Development.

Chomik, R., & Whitehouse, E. R. (2010). *Trends in pension eligibility ages and life expectancy, 1950–2050.* OECD

BIBLIOGRAPHY

Social, Employment and Migration Working Papers No. 105. http://dx.doi.org/10.1787/5km68fzhs2q4-en

Choyce, R. (1992, January). Why become a project management professional? *PM Network*, 32–33.

Cibinic, J., and Nash, R. (1998). *Formation of government contracts* (3rd ed.). Washington, D.C.: CCH, Inc.

Clayton, D., D'Amico, C., & Torpey-Seboe, N. (2019). Back to School? What Adults Without Degrees Say About Pursuing Additional Education and Training. Strada-Gallup Education Consumer Survey Report. Downloaded from https://www.stradaeducation.org/report/back-to-school/.

Cleland, D., Gallagher, J. & Whitehead, R. (1993). *Military project management handbook.* San Francisco, CA: McGraw-Hill.

Cloned cows show no signs of premature aging. (2000, April 27). *News Sentinel,* p. 10.

Collins, M. (2011, March 15). Worker confidence on having enough money for retirement hits 20-year low. *Bloomberg.com.* http://www.bloomberg.com/news/2011-03-15/worker-confidence-on-retirement money-at-20-year-low-ebri-says.html.

Congressional Budget Office (2024). *The Demographic Outlook: 2024 – 2054. Downloaded from www.cbo.gov/publication/59697.*

Coursera. (2019). *Global Skills Index 2019. The World's Top Trending Skills in Business, Technology, and Data Science Benchmarked Across 60 Countries and 10 Industries.* Downloaded from www.coursea.org/gsi.

Christensen, C., & Eyring, H. (2011). *The innovative university: Changing the DNA of higher education from the inside out*. San Francisco, CA: Jossey-Bass.

Cullen, M. (2008). *35 Dumb Things Well-Intended People Say*. Garden City, N.Y., Morgan James Publishing.

Cummings, T. G., & Worley, C. G. (2009). *Organizational development and change* (9th ed.). Mason, OH: South-Western Cengage Learning.

Deloitte (2015). *The Skills Gap in U.S. Manufacturing: 2015 and Beyond*. https://www2.deloitte.com/us/en/pages/manufacturing/articles/boiling-point-the-skills-gap-in-us-manufacturing.html.

Deloitte (2016). Deloitte's 2016 Global Outsourcing Survey. Downloaded from https://www2.deloitte.com/content/dam/Deloitte/nl/Documents/operations/deloitte-nl-s&o-global-outsourcing-survey.pdf.

Dent, H. (2014). *The demographic cliff*. New York: Penguin Group.

Dessler, G. (2000). *Management: Leading people and organizations in the 21st century* (2nd ed.). Upper Saddle River, NJ: Prentice Hall.

Dessler, G. (2011). *Human resource management* (12th ed.). Upper Saddle River, NJ: Prentice Hall.

Dickeson, R. (2010). *Prioritizing academic programs and services: Reallocating resources to achieve strategic balance*. San Francisco, CA: John Wiley & Sons.

Dickler, J. (2012, May 15). *Boomerang kids: 85% of college grads move home*. CNNMoney. Retrieved from http://money.cnn.com/2010/10/14/pf/boomerang_kids_move_home/

Dillow, C. (2011, July). How to make a giant chain gun even deadlier: Give it a laser cannon. *Popular Science Online.* http://www.popsci.com/technology/article/2011-07/ how-make-deadly-chain-gun-even-deadlier-add-laser-cannon

Dimock, M. (2019). Defining Generations: Where Millennials End and Generation Z Begins. Pew Research Center. January 17, 2019.

DOJ (2018). Hate Crime Statistics 2017. Department of Justice, Federal Bureau of Investigations. Downloaded from https://ucr.fbi.gov/hate-crime/2017.

Dolan, K. A. (2006, April 17). Offshoring the offshores. *Forbes,* 75–76.

Doudna, J. & Sternberg, S. (2017). *A Crack in Creation.* New York, NY: Houghton Mifflin Harcourt.

Draut, T. (2005). *Strapped: Why America's 20and 30-some-things can't get ahead.* New York: Doubleday.

Dugas, C. (2011, March 15). More workers have a gloomy retirement outlook. *USA Today,* p. A1.

Dychtwald, K. (1999). *Age power: How the 21st century will be ruled by the new old.* New York: Tarcher Putnam.

Dychtwald, K., Erickson, T. J., & Morison, R. (2006). *Workforce crisis: How to beat the coming shortage of skills and talent.* Boston, MA: Harvard Business School Press.

Dychtwald, M. (2003). *Cycles: How we will live, work and buy.* New York: Free Press.

Dyrenfurth, M., Newton, K., & Springer, M. (2017). Fueling Industry 4.0 – A Professional Doctorate in Technology. European Society for Engineering

Education (SEFI) 2017 Annual Conference Proceedings. Terceira Island, Azores (Portugal).

Dyrenfurth, M., Springer, M., & Newton, K. (2020). In Need of a New Doctorate: A New Population to be Served. ASEE 2020 Annual Conference Proceedings. Montreal, Quebec, Canada.

Ellis, B. (2011, March 15). Most workers have saved just $25,000 for retirement. *CNNMoney.com.* http://money.cnn.com/2011/03/15/retirement/retirement_confidence/index.htm

Encyclopedia Americana. (1996). Danbury, CT: Grolier Incorporated.

Erickson, T. (2008). *Retire Retirement: Career Strategies for the Boomer Generation.* Boston, MA: Harvard Business Press.

Federal Acquisition Regulations System, 48 C.F.R. (2011).

Finn, J. (2008, August 20). The power of older workers. *Inc. 5000.* http://www.inc.com/inc5000/2008/articles/retirees.html

Fishman, T. C. (2005, March 1). How China will change your businesses. *Inc. Magazine.* http://www.inc.com/magazine/20050301/china.html

Fitzgerald, C., & Kirby, L. (Eds.). (1997). *Developing leaders: Research and applications in psychological type and leadership development.* Palo Alto, CA: Davies Black.

Flaherty, C. (2019). *Hot Issues in Graduate and Professional Education.* Inside Higher Education. October 8, 2019.

Fleming, Q. W. (1992). *Cost/schedule control systems criteria: A management guide to C/SCSC* (2nd ed.). Chicago: Probus Publishing Company.

Fortin, P. (2018). How to Fix the Adjunct Crisis. The Chronicle of Higher Education. Downloaded from the internet May 31, 2018. https://www.chronicle.com/article/How-to-Fix-the-Adjunct-Crisis/243535.

Fossel, M., Blackburn, G. & Woynarowski, D. (2011). *The immortality edge: Realizing the secrets of your telomeres for a longer, healthier life.* Hoboken, NJ: John Wiley & Sons, Inc.

Frame, J. D. (1999). *Project management competence: Building key skills for individuals, teams, and organizations.* San Francisco: Jossey-Bass.

Frankel, L. (2004). *Nice Girls Don't Get the Corner Office: 101 Unconscious Mistakes Women Make That Sabotage Their Careers.* New York, NY.: Business Plus.

Frey, R. (1999). *Successful proposal strategies for small businesses: Using knowledge management to win government, private-sector, and international contracts.* Boston: Artech House.

Fry, R. (2018). *More Adults Now Share Their Living Space, Driven in Part by Parents Living with Their Adult Children.* Pew Research Center. January 31. Retrieved from http://www.pewresearch.org/fact-tank/2018/01/31/more-adults-now-share-their-living-space-driven-in-part-by-parents-living-with-their-adult-children/

Frey, W. (2018). The Millennial Generation: A Demographic Bridge to America's Diverse Future. *Metropolitan Policy Program at Brookings.* Downloaded January 2, 2018 from https://www.brookings.edu/research/millennials/.

Frey, W. (2018). Diversity Explosion: How New Racial Demographics Are Remaking America. Washington, D.C., The Brookings Institution.

Fromm, J. & Garton, C. (2013). *Marketing to Millennials.* New York, NY: AMACOM.

Fry, R. (2015). This Year, Millennials will overtake Baby Boomers. *Pew Research Center.* Downloaded Dec 22, 2015 from http://www.pewresearch.org/fact-tank/2015/12/22/15-striking-findings-from-2015/ [12/23/2015 12:44:23 PM].

Fry, R. (2018). *More Adults Now Share Their Living Space, Driven in Part by Parents Living with Their Adult Children.* Pew Research Center. January 31. Retrieved from http://www.pewresearch.org/fact-tank/2018/01/31/more-adults-now-share-their-living-space-driven-in-part-by-parents-living-with-their-adult-children/

Frey, W. (2019). *For the First Time on Record, Fewer Than 10% of Americans Moved in a Year.* Brookings Institute. November 22, 2019.

Frey, W. (2024). *Census Shows America's Post-2020 Population is Driven by Diversity Especially Among the Young.* Brookings. July 24, 2024.

Frey, W. (2025). *Immigration Drives the Nation's Healthy Post-Pandemic Growth.* Brookings. January 6, 2025.

Gao, G. (2015). 15 Striking Findings from 2015. *Pew Research Center.* Downloaded Dec 22, 2015 from http://www.pewresearch.org/fact-tank/2015/12/22/15-striking-findings-from-2015/[12/23/2015 12:44:23 PM]

Gardner, L. (2019). *The Rise of the Mega University.* The Chronicle of Higher Education.

Geiger, A. & Bialik, K. (2019). *The Changing Face of Congress in 6 Charts.* Pew Research Center. February 15, 2019.

Giang, V. (2012). *Why Recent Grads are Moving Back Home in Droves*. Business Insider, September 12, 2012. Downloaded from the internet on September 19, 2014. http://www.businessinsider.com/recent-graduates-heres-some-reasons-to-move-back-home-after-graduation-2012-9

Gibbons, M. T. (2004). *The year in numbers*. Washington, D.C.: American Society of Engineering Education (ASEE).

Gibson, J. L., Ivancevich, J. M., Donnelly, J. H., & Konopaske, R. (2011). *Organizations: Behavior, structure, processes* (14th ed.). New York: McGraw-Hill/Irwin.

Gioia, J. (1992, November). Comprehensive program management. *PM Network*, 5–7.

Goldberg, B. (2000). *Age works: What corporate America must do to survive the graying of the workforce*. New York: Free Press.

Goldstein, L. S. B., & Schneider, M. (2010). *Stem cells for dummies*. Indianapolis, IN: Wiley Publishing Company.

Goleman, D. (1995). *Emotional intelligence*. New York: Bantam Books.

Goleman, D., Boyatzis, R., & McKee, A. (2002). *Primal leadership: Learning to lead with emotional intelligence*. Boston: Harvard Business Review Press.

Gonzalez, V., Ahlman, L., & Fung, A. (2019). *Student Debt and the Class of 2018*. The Institute for College Access and Success. 14th Annual Report. September, 2019.

Grady, J. (1993). *System requirements analysis*. San Francisco, CA: McGraw-Hill.

Grady, J. O. (2010). *Systems management: Planning, enterprise identity, and deployment* (2nd ed.). Boca Raton, FL: CRC Press.

Graff, H. F., & Krout, J. A. (1971). *The adventure of the American people* (3rd ed.). New York: Rand McNally.

Grayson, Jr., C. J., & O'Dell, C. (1988). *American business: A two-minute warning.* New York: Free Press.

Grawe, N, (2018). Demographics and the Demand for Higher Education. Baltimore, MD., Johns Hopkins University Press.

Gurian, M., & Annis, B. (2008). *Leadership and the sexes: Using gender science to create success in business.* San Francisco: Jossey-Bass.

Hadary, S. and Henderson, L. (2013). *How Women Lead: The 8 Essential Strategies Women Know.* New York, NY.: McGraw Hill.Hammer, A. (1993). *Introduction to type and careers.* Washington, D.C.: Consulting Psychologists Press.

Hais, M., & Winograd, M. (2020). The Future is Female: How the Growing Political Power of Women will Remake American Politics. Brookings. https://www.brookings.edu/blog/fixgov/2020/02/19/the-future-is-female-how-the-growing-political-power-of-women-will-remake-american-politics/.

Hankin, H. (2005). *The new workforce: Five sweeping trends that will shape your company's future.* New York: AMACOM.

Hatfield, J. (2025). *The Changing Face of Congress [119th] in 7 Charts.* Pew Research Center. March 3, 2025.

Helman, R., Copeland C., & VanDerhei, J. (2011). *The 2011 Retirement Confidence Survey: Confidence drops to record lows, reflecting the "new normal"* (Issue Brief No. 355). Washington, D.C.: Employee Benefit Research Institute. http://www.ebri.org/pdf/surveys/rcs/2011/ EBRI_03-2011_No355_RCS-11.pdf

Heller, S. (1999). *The Complete Idiot's Guide to Conquering Fear and Anxiety.* New York, N.Y., Macmillan Inc.

Hennigan, W. J. (2011, July 26). Flying robotic seagull attracts flock of birds. *Los Angeles Times, Business.* http://latimesblogs.latimes.com/technology/2011/07/robot-bird-drone-festo-ted.html.

Herman, R., Olivo, T., & Gioia, J. (2003). *Impending crisis: Too many jobs, too few people.* Winchester, VA: Oakhill Press.

Higgins, J. M. (1994). *The management challenge: An introduction to management.* New York: Prentice Hall.

Hoban, F. T. (1992, August). An overview of training and development strategies for NASA project management. *PM Network,* 44–49.

Hodson, S., Phillips, E., & Watson, T. (2024). *Immigration and the Future of Social Security.* Brookings Center for Economic Security and Opportunity.

Horowitz, J., Graf, N., & Livingston, G. (2019). *Marriage and Cohabitation in the U.S.* PEW Research Center. November 19, 2019.

House, J. (2018). *Report: For Many Adult Learners, Going to College is Desirable but Unaffordable.* Education Dive. Retrieved from https://www.educationdive.com/news/report-for-many-adult-learners-going-to-college-is-desirable-but-unafford/514902/

Howard, P. J. (2006). *Owner's manual for the brain: Everyday applications from mind-brain research* (3rd ed.). Austin, TX: Bard Press.

Huntley, R. (2006). *The world according to Y: Inside the new adult generation.* Sydney, Australia: Allen & Unwin.

IASP. (2019). *Stalling Dreams: How Student Debt is Disrupting Life Chances and Widening the Racial Wealth Gap.* Institute on Assets and Social Policy. September 2019.

Indiana Department of Workforce Development, Research & Analysis, Long-term Projections. (2016).

Ingraham, C. (2019). *7 Ways $1.6 Trillion in Student Loan Debt Affects the U.S. Economy.* The Washington Post. June 25, 2019.

Jeffers, S. (1987). *Feel the Fear And Do It Anyway.* New York, NY.: Harcourt Inc.

Jered, S. (2014). *Adjuncts Welcome Congress's New Interest in Their Working Conditions.* The Chronicle of Higher Education. July 30, 2014. Downloaded from the internet on Sep. 22, 2014. http://chronicle.com/article/Adjuncts-Welcome-Congresss/147973/.

Johansson, F. (2004). *The Medici effect: What elephants and epidemics can teach us about innovation.* Boston, MA: Harvard Business School Press.

Johnson, L., & Learned, A. (2004). *Don't think pink: What really makes women buy—and how to increase your share of this crucial market.* New York: AMACOM.

Johnson, M., & Johnson, L., (2010). *Generations, Inc.: From Boomers to Linksters—managing the friction between generations at work.* New York: AMACOM.

Jonas, N. (1986, March 3). The hollow corporation. *BusinessWeek*, 57.

Kamenetz, A. (2006). *Generation debt: Why now is a terrible time to be young.* New York: Riverhead Books.

Karsh, B. & Templin, C. (2013). *Manager 3.0.* New York, NY: AMACOM.Kasworm, C., Rose, A. & Ross-Gordon, J. (2010). *Handbook of adult and continuing education* (2010 ed.). Thousand Oaks, CA: Sage Publications.

Keathley, J., Merrill, P., Owens, T., & Meggarrey, I. (2013). "The Executive Guide to Innovation: Turning Good Ideas into Great Results." Quality Press.Kerzner, H. (2009). *Project management: A systems approach to planning, scheduling and controlling* (10th ed.). Hoboken, NJ: Wiley.

Kelderman, E. (2019). *The Looming Enrollment Crisis: How Colleges are Responding to Shifting Demographics and New Student Needs.* The Chronicle of Higher Education.

Kiley, K. (2011). Where universities can be cut. *Inside Higher Education Online.* Retrieved from http://www.insidehighered.com/news/2011/09/16/unc_berkeley_cornell_experience_show_where_administrativ_cuts_can_be_made

King, C. G. (1992, August). Multi-discipline teams: A fundamental element of the program management process. *PM Network,* 13–22.

Kinsella, K., & Velkoff, V. (2001). *An aging world: 2001* (International Population Reports, Series P95/01-1). Washington, D.C.: U.S. Government Printing Office.

Kirsch, I., Braun, H., Yamamoto, K., & Sum, A. (2007). *America's perfect storm: Three forces changing our nation's future.* Princeton, NJ: Educational Testing Service.

Knowles, M. S., Holton, E. F., & Swanson, R. A. (2011). *The adult learner: The definitive classic in adult education and human resource development* (7th ed.). Burlington, MA: Butterworth-Heinemann.

Kot, F. & Hendel, D. (2012). "Emergence and growth of professional doctorates in the United States, United Kingdom, Canada and Australia: a comparative analysis," *Studies in Higher Education*, Vol. 37, No. 3, 2012, pp. 345-364, DOI: 10.1080/03075079.2010.516356 Available: http://dx.doi.org/10.1080/03075079.2010.516356

Kotlikoff, L. J. 2004. *The coming generational storm: What you need to know about America's economic future.* Cambridge, MA: MIT Press.

Kowalski, T. J. (1988). *The organization and planning of adult education.* Albany, NY: SUNY Press.

Kramer, A., & Harris, A. (2016). Breaking Through Bias: Communication techniques for Women to Succeed at Work. New York, NY: Bibliomotion, Inc.

Krell, E. (2011, June). The global talent mismatch. *HR Magazine*, 68–72.

Kozwolski, K. (2013, July 30). Michigan colleges struggle to attract students: Shrinking pool of high school graduates hits state universities. *The Detroit News Online.*

Ladika, S. (2006, April). The brain race. *HR Magazine*, 69.

Land, R. E. (2012, Spring). Engineering technologists are engineers. *Journal of Engineering Technology.* 32–39.

Lang, R., Alfonso, M., & Dawkins, C. (2009, May). American Demographics—Circa 2109. *Planning*, 10–15.

Last, J. (2013). *What to expect when no one's expecting.* New York: Encounter Books.

Levine, A. and Dean, D. (2013). *Generation on a tightrope.* San Francisco, CA: John Wiley & Sons.

Levinson, D. J. (1978). *The seasons of a man's life.* New York: Ballantine.

Likert, R. (1967). *The human organization: Its management and value.* New York: McGraw-Hill.

Lipman, J. (2018). That's What She Said. New York, N.Y., Harper Collins Publishers.

Lohr, S. (2011, January 1). When innovation, too, is made in China. *New York Times, Business Day.* http://www.nytimes.com/2011/01/02/business/02unboxed.html.

Loo, D. (2011a, July 18). Big pharma launches a talent raid in China. *Bloomberg Businessweek*, 21–22.

Loo, D. (2011b, July 11). Move over Boston, China eyes biotech too. *Bloomberg Businessweek*, 20–21.

Marcel, J. (2000, September 29). A white rabbit that glows in the dark. *The American Reporter, 6*(1430). http://www.ekac.org/amrep.html.

Marcus, J. (2013, July 21). *Like private businesses, universities consolidate to cut costs.* The Hechinger Report. Retrieved from http://nation.time.com/2013/07/19/cash-strapped-universities-turn-to-corporate-style-consolidation/?xid=newsletter-daily.

Marcus, L. (2019). *Some Colleges Seek Radical Solutions to Survive.* Higher Education. October 10, 2019.

Marken, S. (2019). *Half of U.S. Now Consider College Education Very Important.* Gallup.

Marrewa, A. (1998). *The feminine warrior: A woman's guide to verbal, psychological, and physical empowerment.* New York: Kensington.

Marston, C. (2007). *Motivating the "What's in it for me?" workforce: Manage across the generational divide and increase profits.* Hoboken, NJ: Wiley.

Medina, L., Sabo, S., & Vespa, J. (2020). *Living Longer: Historical and Projected Life Expectancy in the United States, 1060-2060.* United States Census Bureau. February 2020.

Memmott, M. (2011, June 15). 2 million 'open jobs'? Yes, but U.S. has a skills mismatch. *The TwoWay: Breaking News from NPR.* http://www.npr.org/blogs/thetwo-way/2011/06/15/137203549/two-million-open-jobs-yes-but-u-s-has-a-skills-mismatch.

Mondy, R., Noe, R. (1993). *Human Resource Management.* Boston, MA. 5th Ed., Allyn and Bacon. Pg. 132.

Montfort, N. (1999, November 1). BioTech (Innovators in the biotechnology industry). *Technology Review, 92.*

Moody's (2013, January 16). *US Higher Education Outlook Negative in 2013.* Industry Outlook, Retrieved from http://www.marquette.edu/budget/documents/USHigherEducationOutlookNegativein2013.pdf

Murk, P. J., & Wells, J. H. (1988, October). A Practical Guide to Program Planning. *Training & Development Journal*, 45–47.

Muschany v. United States. (1994). Retrieved from http://supreme.justia.com/cases/federal/us/324/49/

Naisbitt, J., and Aburdene, P. (1990). *Megatrends 2000: Ten new directions for the 1990's.* New York: Avon Books.

Nahavandi, Afsaneh (2009). *The Art and Science of Leadership* (5th Ed.). Upper Saddle River, NJ: Prentice Hall.

National Academy of Sciences. (2010). *Rising above the gathering storm, revisited: Rapidly approaching Category 5.* Washington, D.C.: National Academies Press

National Academy of Sciences. (2012). Research Universities and the Future of America: Ten Breakthrough Actions Vital to our Nation's Prosperity and Security. Washington, D.C.: National Academies Press.

National Center for Education Statistics. (2022). Glossary: Doctor's Degree-Professional Practice. (n.d.). Available: https://nces.ed.gov/ipeds/glossary/index.asp?id=942

National Federation of Independent Business (NFIB). (2011). The benefits of hiring semi-retired workers. *NFIB.com.* http://www.nfib.com/business-resources/business-resources-item?cmsid=50011

National Human Genome Research Institute (NHGRI). (2007). A guide to your genome. *National Human Genome Research Institute.* http://www.genome.gov/Pages/Education/AllAbouttheHumanGenome Project/GuidetoYourGenome07.pdf

National Institutes of Health (NIH). (n.d.). Human genome project fact sheet. *National Institutes of Health.* http://report.nih.gov/nihfactsheets/ViewFactSheet.aspx?csid=45&key=H.

National Science Foundation (NSF). (2006). *Science and engineering indicators 2006.* Arlington, VA: National Science Foundation.

National Science Foundation (NSF). (2010). *Science and engineering indicators 2010.* Arlington, VA: National Science Foundation.

National Science Foundation (NSF). (2014). *Science and engineering indicators 2014*. Arlington, VA: National Science Foundation.

National Science Foundation (NSF). (2016). *Science and engineering indicators 2016*. Arlington, VA: National Science Foundation.

National Science Foundation (NSF). (2018). *Science and engineering indicators 2018*. Arlington, VA: National Science Foundation.

National Science Foundation (NSF). (2020). *Science and engineering indicators 2020*. Arlington, VA: National Science Foundation.

National Science Foundation (NSF). (2022). *Science and engineering indicators 2022*. Arlington, VA: National Science Foundation.

National Science Foundation (NSF). (2024). *Science and engineering indicators 2024*. Arlington, VA: National Science Foundation.

Newton, K. (2017). Proposal for a Doctor of Technology Degree. Unpublished proposal submitted to Purdue University Graduate School. West Lafayette, IN. April 2017.

Newton, K., Springer, M., & Dyrenfurth, M. (2019). The Professional Doctorate in Technology Leadership, Research & Innovation. ASEE 2019 Annual Conference Proceedings. Tampa, FL.

Newton, K., Springer, M., & Dyrenfurth, M. (2021). Needs and Goals of Professional Doctoral Students in Technology. ASEE 2021 Annual Conference Proceedings. Long Beach, California.

Norman, Carter, H. (1986, Summer). Guaranteeing management's future through succession planning. *Journal of Information Systems Management*, 19.

Oberhauser, A. (2021). Women is the US are Having Fewer Babies. What's Driving this Trend?. World Economic Forum. July 2021.

Oliver, R. W. (2000). *The coming biotech age: The business of bio-materials.* New York: McGraw Hill.

Organisation for Economic Co-operation and Development (OECD). (2011). Pensions at a glance 2011: Retirement income systems in OECD and G20 countries. *OECD Publishing.* http://dx.doi.org/10.1787/pension_glance-2011-en.

Organisation for Economic Co-operation and Development (OECD). (2017). OECD Science, Technology and Industry Scoreboard 2017: The Digital Transformation. *OECD Publishing.* Download from http://www.oecd-ilibrary.org/docserver/download/9217081e.pdf?expires=1513618366&id=id&accname=guest&checksum=4C206F99AF42AD6F554A2723C9ECC63D.

Overly, S. (2011, June 19). For science and tech companies, immigration debate strikes a different tone. *The Washington Post, Capital Business.* http://www.washingtonpost.com/...ness/capitalbusiness/forscience-and-tech-companies-immigration-debate-strikes-a-different-tone/2011/06/16/AGmWoxbH_ story.html

Panetta, G. & Lee, S. (2019). Meet the 116th Congress. Business Insider, Jan. 5, 2019. Downloaded from https://www.businessinsider.com/changes-in-gender-racial-diversity-between-the-115th-and-116th-house-2018-12.

Paquette, D. (2004). Dichotomizing Paternal and Maternal Functions as a Means to Better Understand Their Primary Contribution. *Human Development*, vol. 47(4), pp. 237-238.

Park, A. (2011, June 13). Cracking cancer's code: Tumor DNA holds the key to beating the disease. *Time*, 69–71.

Parker, K, Graf, N. & Igielnik, R. (2019). Generation Z Looks a Lot Like Millennials on Key Social and Political Issues. Pew Research Center. January 17, 2019.

Pearson. (2019). *The Global Learner Survey*. Pearson. September 2019.

PEW Research Center. (2008). *Men or women: Who's the better leader?* Retrieved from http://www.pewsocialtrends.org/2008/08/25/men-or-women-whos-the-better-leader/

PEW Research Center (2011, December 14). *Barely half of U.S. adults are married: A record low*. Pew Research Center Report.

PEW Research Center (2012, February 9). *Young, underemployed and optimistic*. Pew Research Center Report. Retrieved from http://www.pewsocialtrends.org/2012/02/09/young-underemployed-and-optimistic/

PEW Research Center (2018). U.S. Immigration – Lessons 1-5. Pew Research Center.

Plunkett, J. (2010). *The next boom: What you absolutely, positively have to know about the world between now and 2025*. Houston, TX: BizExecs Press.

PMI (2013). *Project Management Institute Jordan Chapter*. Retrieved from http://www.pmi-jo.org/public/English.aspx?Lang=3&Page_Id=211.

Pollack, A. (2011, May 18). *A blood test offers clues to longevity.* New York Times, Business Day. http://www.nytimes.com/2011/05/19/business/19life.html?pagewanted=all

Powell, B. (2011, June 27). The end of cheap labor in China. *Time*, 1–4.

Price, M. T. (1992, October). A process approach to project manager training. *PM Network*, 17–26.

Project Management Institute. (2025). *Job Growth and Talent Gap 2017 – 2027.* Project Management Institute. Report # 2017-2027.

Project Management Institute. (2025). *Talent Gap. 10-Year Employment Trends, Costs, and Employment Implications.* Project Management Institute. June 2021.

Project Management Institute. (2025). *Narrowing the Talent Gap.* Project Management Institute. 2021.

Project Management Institute. (2025). *Project Management Salary Survey. 13th edition.* Project Management Institute. 2023.

Puliyenthuruthel, J., & Kripalani, M. (2005, February 14). India: Good help is hard to find. *BusinessWeek*, 52.

Ratanjee, V. & Green, A. (2018). How to Reduce Bias in Your Succession and Promotion Plans. Gallup, Inc. Downloaded from https://news.gallup.com/business-journal/235436/poll/232319/facebook-users-privacy-concerns-2011.aspx.

Rathe, J. (2010, January 9). The perception that older workers are less productive than younger ones is false. *RetiredBrains.com.* http://retiredbrains.blogspot.com/2010/01/perception-that-older-workers-are- less.html

Rawe, J. (2000, May 22). Economy. *Time Magazine, 155*(21), 21–22.

Reina, D., & Reina, M. (2015). *Trust and betrayal in the workforce* (3rd ed.). Oakland, CA: Berrett-Koehler.

Reinhardt, A. (2006, January 30). Angling to be the next Bangalore. *BusinessWeek,* 62.

Robbins, S. (1998). *Organizational behavior: concepts, controversies, applications* (8th ed.). Upper Saddle River, NJ: Prentice Hall.

Robbins, S. (1999). *Management* (5th ed.). Upper Saddle River, NJ: Prentice Hall.

Rosenburg, N., & Birdzell, L. E. (1986). *How the West grew rich: The economic transformation of the industrial world.* New York: Basic Books.

Ross, H. (2014). Everyday Bias: Identifying and Navigating Unconscious Judgments in Our Daily Lives. New York, N.Y., Rowman & Littlefield.

Ross, H., Tartaglione, J. & Cole, J. (2018) Our Search for Belonging: How Our Need to Connect is Tearing Us Apart. New York, N.Y., Berrett-Koehler Publishers.

Rothwell, W. J. (2010). *Effective Succession Planning: Ensuring leadership continuity and building talent from within.* New York: AMACOM.

Rue, L. W., & Byars, L. L. (1989). *Management: Theory and Application* (5th ed.). Homewood, IL: Irwin.

Ruskin, A. M. (1992, April). Concerns of project managers: Project risk management. *PM Network,* 30–37.

Sacks, D. (2006, January/February). Scenes from the culture clash. *Fast Company,* 73–75.

Saeed, J. (2018). 3 Enrollment Pressures to Prepare for in 2018. Education Advisory Board (EAB). Retrieved from https://www.eab.com/research-and-insights/academic-affairs-forum/expert-insights/2018/2018-challenges-for-academic-affairs.

Santrock, J. W. (1999). *Life-Span Development* (7th ed.). New York: McGraw Hill.

Saunders, N. (2005, November 5). A summary of BLS projections to 2014. *Monthly Labor Review.* http://www.bls.gov/opub/mlr/2005/11/art1full.pdf

Scarborough, N. M. (1992). *Business: Gaining the competitive edge.* Needham Heights, MA: Allyn & Bacon.

Schuster, S. (2011, June 28). Genetic sequencing may aid survival of Tasmanian devil. *USA Today,* 9A.

Seaman, D. F., & Fellenz, R. A. (1989). *Effective strategies for teaching adults.* Columbus, OH: Merrill Publishing.

Seemiller, C. & Grace, M. (2016). *Generation Z Goes to College.* San Francisco, CA.: Jossey-Bass.

Selingo, J. (2013). *College (UN) bound.* Boston, MA: New Harvest.

Selingo, J. (2016). *2026 the Decade Ahead – The Seismic Shifts Transforming the Future of Higher Education.* The Chronicle of Higher Education, Inc.

Selingo, J., Carey, K., Pennington, H., Fishman, R., & Palmer, I. (2013, May). *The next generation university.* New America Foundation. Retrieved from http://higheredwatch.newamerica.net/blogposts/2013/the_next_generation_university-84378

Selingo, J. (2017). *2026 The Decade Ahead: The Seismic Shifts Transforming the Future of Higher Education.* The Chronicle of Higher Education Report.

Serruya, M. D., Hatsopoulos, N. G., Paninski, L., Fellows, M. R., & Donoghue, J. P. (2002). Instant neural control of a movement signal. *Nature, 416*(6877), 141–142.

Scott, C., & Jaffe, D. (2009). Managing Personal Change: Stay Positive and Stay in Control. 3rd Ed. New York, NY: Axzo Press.

Scott, M. & Nightingale, D. (2018). The Education-Jobs "Mix-Match": How Much Opportunity is There for the College-Educated Workforce in America's Metropolitan Areas? Urban Institute. Washington, D.C.

Sheehy, G. (1998). *Understanding men's passages: Discovering the new map of men's lives.* New York: Random House.

Shelton, C., & Shelton, L. (2005). *The neXt revolution: What gen X women want at work and how their Boomer bosses can help them get it.* Mountain View, CA: Davies-Black.

Shenkar, O. (2005). *The Chinese century: The rising Chinese economy and its impact on the global economy, the balance of power, and your job.* Upper Saddle River, NJ: Wharton.

SkillSurvey. (2019). The Future of Work and Generation Z: The Data You Need For More Strategic Recruiting. SkillSurvey. September 26, 2019, downloaded from https://www.skillsurvey.com/resource/generation-z-in-the-workplace-ebook/.

Smith, C., Turner, S. (2016). *The Radical Transformation of Diversity and Inclusion: The Millennial Influence.*

BIBLIOGRAPHY

Deloitte University, The Leadership Center for Inclusion. Downloaded from https://www2.deloitte.com/us/en/pages/about-deloitte/articles/radical-transformation-of-diversity-and-inclusion.html.

Smith, G. (2008 May 21). Mexico: Pumping out engineers. *BusinessWeek.* http://www.businessweek.com/stories/2006-05-21/mexico-pumping-out-engineers

Smith, P. (1986). *Taking charge: A practical guide for leaders.* Washington, D.C.: National Defense University Press.Smith, J. W., & Clurman, A. (1997). *Rocking the ages: The Yankelovich report on generational marketing.* New York: Harper Business.

Social Security Administration (SSA). (2005). *Social Security: A Brief History.* Washington, D.C.: Social Security Administration. http://www.ssa.gov/history/pdf/2005pamphlet.pdf

Sorrel, C. (2011, July 26). IBM's mighty morphin' touchscreen keyboard tailors itself to your hands. *Wired Online.* http://www.wired.com/gadgetlab/2011/07/ibms-mighty-morphin-touchscreen-keyboard-tailors-itself-to-your-hands

Springer, M. L. (2005). *A concise guide to program management: Fundamental concepts and issues.* West Lafayette, IN: Purdue University Press.

Springer, M. L. (2013). *Project and program management: A competency-based approach* (2nd ed.). West Lafayette, IN: Purdue University Press.

Springer, M. L. (2016). *Project and program management: A competency-based approach* (3rd ed.). West Lafayette, IN: Purdue University Press.

Springer, M. L. (2019). Project and Program Management: A Competency-Based Approach. 4th ed. West Lafayette, IN: Purdue University Press.

Springer, M. L. (2023). Project and Program Management: A Competency-Based Approach. 5th ed. West Lafayette, IN: Purdue University Press.

Springer, M. L. (2019a). The Design, Development, and Implementation of a Doctor of Technology Degree Program. Indiana Council for Continuing Education (ICCE) Annual Conference 2019. Indianapolis, IN.

Springer, M. L. (2019b). Social, Political and Economic Cultural Perspectives and Implications of America's Two Youngest Cohorts: Gen Y (Millennials) and Gen Z. Indiana Council for Continuing Education (ICCE) Annual Conference 2019. Indianapolis, IN. Presentation Accepted. Conference Postponed.

Springer, M. L. (2019c). The Changing Face of Higher Education. ASEE Conference for Industry and Education Collaboration (CIEC) 2019 Conference. New Orleans, LA.

Springer, M. L. (2019d). Recognizing the Diversity Transformation of U.S. Demographics. ASEE Conference for Industry and Education Collaboration (CIEC) 2019 Conference. New Orleans, LA.

Springer, M. L. (2019e). The Changing Face of Higher Education. ASEE Conference for Industry and Education Collaboration (CIEC) 2019 Conference. New Orleans, LA.

Springer, M. L. (2019f). Recognizing the Diversity Transformation of U.S. Demographics. ASEE Conference for Industry and Education Collaboration (CIEC) 2019 Conference. New Orleans, LA.

Springer, M. L. (2020). Why Don't You Like Me? Unconscious Bias and the Changing Mosaic of Our Nation. Lafayette, IN: Niche Pressworks.

Springer, M., Bertoline, G., & Schuver, M. (2011b). Building an Academic Center Infrastructure for Professional Development. In *Proceedings of the 2011 American Society for Engineering Education Annual Conference*. Washington, D.C.: American Society for Engineering Education.

Springer, M., & Newton, K. (2019). Changing U.S. Age, Racial and Ethnic Demographics and Its Impact on Higher Education. ASEE 2019 Annual Conference Proceedings. Tampa, FL.

Springer, M. L., & Schuver, M. T. (2014). Creating Synergistic Opportunities for Professional Adult Continuing Learners Through Engineering and Technology Collaborations. *ASEE 2014 Annual Conference Proceedings*. Indianapolis, IN.

Springer, M. L., & Schuver, M. T. (2015). The New Professional Working Adult Learner – The Next Generational Cohort. *ASEE 2015 Annual Conference Proceedings*. Seattle, WA.

Springer, M. L., & Schuver, M. T. (2016). A Return on Investment Force Multiplier of an Entrepreneurial Administrative Organization for Professional Studies. *ASEE 2016 Annual Conference Proceedings*. New Orleans, LA.

Springer, M. L., & Schuver, M. T. (2018). Dwindling Graduate Student Enrollments in Distance-Based Programs: A Research-Based Exploration with Findings and Underlying Premise. *ASEE 2018 Annual Conference Proceedings*. Salt Lake City, UT.

Springer, M. L., Schuver, M. T., & Dyrenfurth, M. J. (2011a). Long term alumnus performance and evaluation after graduation from a distance learning hybrid weekend master's degree program in technology. *ASEE 2011 Annual Conference Proceedings.* Vancouver, B.C.

Springer, M. L., Schuver, M. T., & Dyrenfurth, M. J. (2011c). Long term alumnus performance and evaluation after graduation from a distance learning hybrid weekend master's degree program in technology. In *Proceedings of the 2011 American Society for Engineering Education Annual Conference.* Washington, D.C.: American Society for Engineering Education.

Sternberg, S. (2011, June 28). The Pitch for Stem Cells. *USA Today*, 1A.

Stinnett, W. D. (1992, May). Lone wolf teams: Reconciling the need for collaboration with the need for individual accomplishment. *PM Network*, 21–25.

Stokes, D. (1997). *Pasteur's quadrant: Basic science and technological innovation.* Harrisonburg, VA: The Brookings Institution.

Stone, L. (2018). The Decline of American Fertility. *Fortune Magazine.* February 1, 2018. P. 16.

Strauss, W., & Howe, N. (1991). *Generations: The history of America's future, 1584 to 2069.* New York: William Morrow and Co.

Student Loan Hero. (2018). A Look at the Shocking Student Loan Debt Statistics for 2018. Student Loan Hero. Downloaded from https://studentloanhero.com/student-loan-debt-statistics/.

Tavernise, S., Miller, C., Quoctrung, B., & Gebeloff, R. (2021). *Why American Women Everywhere are Delaying Motherhood.* The New York Times. September 30, 2021.

Tavernise, S. (2021). *The U.S. Birthrate has Dropped Again. The Pandemic May be Accelerating the Decline.* The New York Times. May 5, 2021.

Taylor, P., Kochhar, R., Morin, R., Wang, W., Dockterman, D., & Medina, J. (2009). *America's changing workforce: Recession turns a graying office grayer.* Washington, D.C.: Pew Research Center. http://pewsocialtrends.org/files/2010/10/americas-changing-workforce.pdf

TFAI. (2019). *Second Place America? Increasing Challenges to U.S. Scientific Leadership.* A Report by the Task Force on American Innovation. May, 2019.

Tulgan, B. (2009). *Not everyone gets a trophy: How to manage Generation Y.* San Francisco: Jossey-Bass.

Twenge, J. M. (2006). *Generation me: Why today's young American's are more confident, assertive, entitled—and more miserable than ever before.* New York: Free Press

Twenge, J. (2017). *iGen.* New York, N.Y.: Simon and Schuster Inc.

United Nations (2011, May 3). World population to reach 10 billion by 2100 if fertility in all countries converges to replacement level. *United Nations Press Release.* http://esa.un.org/unpd/wpp/other-information/Press_Release_WPP2010.pdf

U.S. Bureau of Labor Statistics. (2013). *Current population survey employment projections.* Retrieved from http://www.bls.gov/emp/ep_chart_001.htm

U.S. Census Bureau (2018). Older People Projected to Outnumber Children for First Time in U.S. History. United States Census Bureau, March 13, 2018. Release Number CB18-41.

Van Alstyne, W. (1993) W. *Freedom and Tenure in the Academy*. Durham, NC: Duke University Press.

Van Fleet, D. D., & Peterson, T. O. (1994). *Contemporary Management* (3rd ed.). Boston: Houghton Mifflin.

Van Horne, C. (2013). *Working Scared (or not at all): the Lost Decade, Great Recession, and Restoring the Shattered American Dream*. Lanham, MA: The Rowman & Littlefield Publishing Group.Vance, A. (2011, May 2). Pacific Biosciences' $600 million decoder ring. *Businessweek*, 57–59.

Vandeveer, R. (2011, April). *Alternative model proposed during a brainstorming session*. Technology Leadership and Innovation (TLI) Combined Advisory Board Meeting. West Lafayette, Indiana.

Veale, J. (2009, February 10). South Korea's pet clone wars. *Time World*. http://www.time.com/time/world/article/0,8599,1878398,00.html

Vergano, D. (1999, May 25). Of transgenic mice and men. *USA Today*, 11D.

Vergano, D. (2012, May 16). Paralysis victims use brain signals to control robotic arm. *USA Today*. http://www.usatoday.com/news/health/story/2012-05-15/robotic-arm/55004238/1?csp=34news.

Vespa, J., Armstrong, D., and Medina, L. (2018). Demographic Turning Points for the United States: Population Projections for 2020 to 2060. Current population Reports, P25-1144, U.S. Census Bureau, Washington, DC.

Wallace, P. (1999). *Agequake: Riding the demographic rollercoaster shaking business, finance, and our world.* London: Nicholas Brealey Publishing.

Waters, R. (2011, March 21). A sales surge for gene sequencing machines. *Businessweek,* 58–60.

Weiss, R. (2000, October 14). Science nears revival of dead species. *Washington Post,* p. 10.

Weldon, L. (2014). *Off Track: Current Number of Tenure, Tenure-Track Faculty Lacking Women.* The Purdue University Exponent. April 8, 2014, pg. 1.

Welsh, A. (1992, May). The future of project management. *PM Network,* 5–6.

Wessel, D. (2013). Four ideas to fix higher education. *The Wall Street Journal Online.* Retrieved from http://online.wsj.com/article/SB10001424127887323971204578626123435046376.html

WICHE (2012). Knocking at the college door: Projections of high school graduates. Report from the Western Interstate Commission of Higher Education. Retrieved from http://www.wiche.edu/knocking-8th

Wikipedia. (2019). downloaded from https://en.wikipedia.org/wiki/Blind_spot_(vision).

Wilson, J. (2000, October). Science's greatest unsolved mysteries. *Popular Mechanics, 177*(10), 52–57.

Woolhouse, M. (2011, January 23). Underemployed and overeducated—and maybe the nation's best hope. *Boston Globe.* http://www.boston.com/business/articles/2011/01/23/study_tempers_pessimism_over_worker_shortage/

World Economic Forum (WEF). (2011). *Global talent risk—Seven responses.* Geneva, Switzerland: World Economic Forum. http://www3.weforum.org/docs/PS_WEF_GlobalTalentRisk_Report_2011.pdf

Young, E. (2000, October 7). Cash cow. *New Scientist.* Retrieved from http://www.newscientist.com/article/dn50-cash-cow.html

Yukl, G. (2002). *Leadership in Organizations* (5th ed.). Upper Saddle River, NJ: Prentice Hall.

Zahneis, M. (2020), The Latest Assault on Tenure. The Chronicle of Higher Education. February 16, 2020. https://www.chronicle.com/article/The-Latest-Assault-on-Tenure/248058.

Zakaria, F. (2011, June). Innovate better: Everyone agrees it's key to America's future. But where do we focus innovation, and how do we fund it?. *Time Magazine,* 30–32.

Zakaria, F. (2012). *The post-American world: Release 2.0.* New York: W. W. Norton.

Zells, L. (1992, May). Applying Japanese total quality management to software project management. *PM Network,* 32–35.

Zemke, R., Raines, C., & Filipczak, B. (2000). *Generations at work: Managing the clash of Veterans, Boomers, Xers, and Nexters in your workplace.* New York: AMACOM.

Zang, S. (2015). *Everything You Need to Know About CRISPR: The New Tool That Edits DNA.* GIZMODO. Retrieved from https://gizmodo.com/everything-you-need-to-know-about-crispr-the-new-tool-1702114381.

Zusman, A. (2013). "Degrees of change: How New Kinds of Professional Doctorates are Changing Higher

Education Institutions," *Research & Occasional Paper Series*: CSHE.8.13. June 2013, Berkeley, CA, USA: University of California, Berkeley. Available: http://eric.ed.gov/?id=ED545185 ERIC Number: ED545185

About the Author

Dr. Mitchell L. Springer
PMP, SPHR, SHRM-SCP

Dr. Springer has extensive theoretical and practical experience based on the defense industry and subsequently higher education spanning four disciplines: software engineering, systems engineering, program management and human resources. He possesses significant strength in pattern recognition, analyzing and improving organizational systems, with expertise in program/project management, organizational restructuring, change management, negotiation, and mediation processes.

Dr. Springer is an internationally recognized scholar and award-winning educator. He has contributed to scholarship more than 400 books, articles, presentations, editorials, and reviews. He is the recipient of numerous awards and recognitions, including local, regional, and national recognitions for leadership in diversity, equity, and inclusion (DEI), with over 100 attendant contributions to DEI scholarship.

Dr. Springer is the Past-President of the Indiana Council for Continuing Education as well as the Past-Chair of the Continuing Professional Development Division of the American Society for Engineering Education (ASEE). He serves as a Division Delegate to the ASEE Commission on DEI. Dr. Springer sits on university and community boards and advisory committees.

Dr. Springer received his Bachelor of Science in Computer Science from Purdue University, his MBA, and Doctorate in Adult and Community Education with a Cognate in Executive Development from Ball State University. He is certified as a Project Management Professional (PMP), Senior Professional in Human Resources (SPHR), SHRM Senior Certified Professional (SCP), in Alternate Dispute Resolution (ADR), and, in civil and domestic mediation. Dr. Springer is a State of Indiana Registered domestic mediator and member of the Indiana Association of Mediators.